Psyche, Soul, and Spirit

Psyche, Soul, and Spirit
Interdisciplinary Essays

Rachel Berghash
and
Katherine Jillson

FOREWORD BY
John L. Kuehn

RESOURCE *Publications* • Eugene, Oregon

PSYCHE, SOUL, AND SPIRIT
Interdisciplinary Essays

Copyright © 2016 Rachel Berghash and Katherine Jillson. All rights reserved. Except for brief quotations in critical publications or reviews, no part of this book may be reproduced in any manner without prior written permission from the publisher. Write: Permissions, Wipf and Stock Publishers, 199 W. 8th Ave., Suite 3, Eugene, OR 97401.

Cover Art & Design: Mark Berghash, copyright © 2016.

Chapter 4, "Milarepa and Demons: Aids to Spiritual and Psychological Growth," was originally published in the *Journal of Religion and Health* 40/3 (Fall 2001) 371–82. Copyright © 2001 Blanton-Peale Institute. Used with kind permission from Springer Science + Business Media.

Chapter 7, "Jeremiah: Creative Advance," was originally published in *Eretz Acheret* 22 (June–July 2004) 82–85. Translated by Yaniv Farkash. Copyright © 2004 by the publisher. Used with permission.

Chapter 8, "Thoughts on Psyche, Soul, and Spirit," was originally published in the *Journal of Religion and Health* 37/4 (Winter 1998) 313–22. Copyright © 1998 Blanton-Peale Institute. Used with kind permission from Springer Science + Business Media.

Resource Publications
An Imprint of Wipf and Stock Publishers
199 W. 8th Ave., Suite 3
Eugene, OR 97401

www.wipfandstock.com

PAPERBACK ISBN: 978-1-4982-2030-9
HARDCOVER ISBN: 978-1-4982-2032-3

Manufactured in the U.S.A.

To Preston, our inspired and beloved teacher

Spirit is merciful and tender because it has no private motive to make it spiteful.

—George Santayana

What lies behind us and what lies before us are tiny matters compared to what lies within us.

—Ralph Waldo Emerson

CONTENTS

Foreword by John L. Kuehn | ix

1. Exploring Unity and Distinction | 1
2. St. Teresa of Avila: Enduring Suffering for One's Values | 15
3. Being and the Self: I Am, but Who Am I? | 28
4. Milarepa and Demons: Aids to Spiritual and Psychological Growth | 43
5. Milarepa on Detachment and Worldliness | 57
6. Subtleties of the Spirit | 66
7. Jeremiah: Creative Advance | 75
8. Thoughts on Psyche, Soul, and Spirit | 84
9. Zoroastrian Prayers and the Character of America | 96
10. The Israeli/Palestinian Conflict: A New Beginning | 101

Bibliography | 121

FOREWORD

THIS BOOK IS DEDICATED to our great late teacher, the psychiatrist and psychoanalyst Preston G. McLean, in the hopes that he will not be forgotten. He died an early death of Alzheimer's disease. Unfortunately he is remembered by only a few students and patients. He is probably the finest psychiatrist no one heard of.

In the United States, there is a notable decline in the practice of religion and the teaching of philosophy and other humanities. Physicalism is in the ascendency. This is the view that the physical or material world is the real world—that nothing exists outside of it—and lots of scientists and some philosophers ascribe to some form of it.

Dr. McLean was a pioneer in introducing the idea of reading and discussing sources of interdisciplinary material—religion, philosophy, psychology, biology, and poetry—and applying them to everyday life. By applying the ideas we enrich the ideas themselves as well as our own lives. He taught all the great religions, different schools of philosophy, and psychoanalysis, with the idea that a particular school will cover some parts of the horizon and not other parts.

Rachel, Katherine, and I met as a result of our being students of Dr. McLean. I first met him—and he took me under his wing—when he returned home to Louisiana in the late sixties. He lectured to us at Louisiana State University (LSU) on psychoanalysis, religion, and health. My colleagues Rachel and Katherine were students of his in New York City during the period when he was the psychiatric consultant to the American Foundation of Religion and Psychiatry. He was also the author of "Philosophy and Psychiatry," in the *American Handbook of Psychiatry*, and, in addition to his medical practice, he taught interdisciplinary seminars on the interior and the instinctual life.

FOREWORD

Dr. McLean's notion of interior life had a broader view than that of the traditional religious concept: "Interior life is autonomous; its connection with religion is accidental. It has to do with the methodology, and the logic, and the psychology of excellence." In his view, the interior life also includes a prayer life and contemplation, developing a capacity for self-support and self-companioning on the basis of having a good conscience, self-discipline, and a solid grounding in philosophy. Philosophy is needed in order to make necessary distinctions between concepts under discussion, clearing up confusions that occur otherwise. For instance, not distinguishing between religion and spirituality results in losing the value of each.

This book, then, is a collection of interdisciplinary essays inspired by the interior life seminar work. Although to the casual observer it may seem to be excessively idiosyncratic or overly intellectual, there are many ideas in here that are helpful to people struggling to make sense out of their lives, and, indeed, to prepare for life and death. The notions in this book are meant to be explored further. The book can be thought of as a receptacle, open to additional original thought.

The authors of this book use a unique approach to material from the various disciplines mentioned above. They "speak the language" of each religion, in contexts in which they have meaning and use for everyday life. What we have here is a methodology—not a system—for developing one's interior life by being open to new ideas, and getting permission and examples from the readings to go beyond one's own intellectual, religious, and spiritual worlds.

According to Dr. McLean, one's *religion* is what one believes in and how these beliefs inform one's day-to-day conduct. Religion (the root word for religion is *religio,* meaning a bind) is characterized as the "housekeeping and bookkeeping" of one's life, with the goal of securing and promoting home, future, repose, and rest. In contrast, the spiritual aspect—the spirit—wanders and is at home wherever it is, reposes and rests in whatever it is contemplating, and is result-free and future-free. One's spiritual life can be enlarged by the study of the spirituality in other religions, where one can find contrast, but also correspondence—the great saint can be a saint in any religion.

A few examples will give the reader a chance to glimpse the spiritual component in this book. St. Teresa, for example, emphasizes many notions, one of which stirs us to think about how often we close ourselves to grace, sometimes in order to avoid attacks from the outside world and

FOREWORD

from within oneself. It also stresses that if we remain relentless in pursuing our spiritual goal, the world will still attack us and we will still suffer, but for our *own* values. What is inspiring in Teresa's example for a religious or lay person is her ability to lead a contemplative and active life, with great courage and persistence in following her values, while dealing with severe internal and external opposition. Milarepa, the Buddhist, is attacked by demons and uses his demons to strengthen himself in his spiritual growth; these processes have psychological equivalents.

The essay on psyche, soul, and spirit points out that these three words are often used interchangeably, lacking distinction. A philosophical discussion studded with examples clarifies the confusion. The essay on Milarepa's detachment from his ego and his renunciation of the world may, from a Western point of view, appear radical, but what is kept in mind is healthy detachment. Milarepa may help deal with our own healthy detachments and unhealthy detachments in their spiritual and psychological meanings.

The authors include as an addendum an essay on the Israeli and Palestinian conflict. Though the essay is political—essentially a political plea—it is driven by psychological, moral, ethical, religious, and spiritual ideas.

Despite it sometimes being a "hard read," I hope many people will give this book a try. It is especially recommended to physicians, the clergy, and others working in the mental health movement—particularly with depressed and anxious patients. It goes without saying that these essays can benefit the general public in addition to professionals.

John L. Kuehn, MD

1
EXPLORING UNITY AND DISTINCTION

Religious study focuses on the unity of the divine and earthly realms: the unity between the individual and God, the unity within an individual and between individuals. On the other hand, philosophers have always proceeded by making distinctions in order to clarify how we experience the world. It is useful to understand the distinctions between religions and to not short-circuit the steps towards unity expressed in the spiritual heights where all religions may meet. However, distinctions can harden and become hierarchical. They can assert themselves to such an extent that we are prevented from seeing important connections.

Another danger of overstating distinctions is separating one's self from the other. When making distinctions leads to an exaggerated sense of identity, one doesn't give room to another point of view. The tendency is to cling to one's own side, hoping to dominate and eclipse the other side, which can be experienced as a threat to one's existence, a threat to be eliminated. Feeling utterly distinct can manifest itself as a bias that claims that other individuals and other nations are inferior. The psychoanalyst Michael Eigen says, "Surely the feeling of wholeness can be dangerous. Fascism makes people feel whole. The sense of wholeness makes people kill each other. My wholeness is right, yours wrong."[1] Here wholeness is intolerant of fracture or dissent. But Eigen points to a more evolved wholeness, a wholeness in the spirit of the Hasidic dictum of Rabbi Nachman: "There is nothing more whole than a broken heart." When wholeness is expansive it embraces distinctions. The whole person has the capacity to be shattered, and not run from it.

Eigen has coined the striking term "distinction-union." He has put together these two parallel tendencies and describes how they coexist despite being oppositional and sometimes mutually destructive. Not only can the urge towards unity and the impulse to make distinctions coexist,

---

1. Eigen, *Mystic*, 52.

they can work together and even nourish each other. Distinction-union is a structure made up of various ways of distinction and various ways of union—linking, fusing, melding, connecting.[2]

Hasidic masters influenced by Kabbalistic thought are credited with an ability to intuit hidden connections between things, connections that lie beyond the boundaries of time and space. The expansiveness of their vision touched the souls of their disciples, regenerating their bodies and their lives by diminishing the distance between them and others, and between them and the divine.[3]

Through concentration and deep experience, and through scientific research, we discover hidden interconnections, dependencies, and interdependencies. We discover unities between entities that we initially perceive as separate. Everything exists in itself, yet everything participates in everything. Eigen highlights our capacity to be connected yet separate; to be in union yet distinct. Indeed, this is a "creative challenge of our nature,"[4] a challenge that we meet with persistence and plasticity. What we experience and the way we experience it makes us who we are. Failure to tolerate two contrary states can result in the disavowing of one of the states, splitting it off and even killing it. This causes pain and suffering, because the rejected state never really dies; it reasserts itself, afflicting body and mind. Equally important is how splitting off parts of ourselves impoverishes us. The capacity to meet the challenge—to hold and tolerate distinct opposing features of ourselves and not feel that brokenness is a threat to our wholeness—speaks to our core, nourishes and enriches us, and gives birth to something new and unexpected.

The psychological aspect of integration sheds light on unity. The psychoanalyst Melanie Klein writes about the longing for an unconscious missing part in one's self. She underscores loneliness rooted in insecurity as a result of longing for the unconscious missing part, the destructive impulses that one has split off and projected onto the other to avoid feeling pain. Acknowledging and integrating this missing part requires a benign superego, which leads to tolerance of shortcomings of oneself and others. This gives room for hate, envy, and other negative feelings, whose impact is lessened when not judged harshly.[5]

---

2. Eigen, online workshop.
3. Buber, *Tales*, 1:11–12.
4. Eigen, *Contact*, 16.
5. Klein, "On the Sense of Loneliness," 300.

EXPLORING UNITY AND DISTINCTION

According to Eigen, an example of distinction-union is seeing faith and catastrophe not as contrary but as connected. Our existence is a mixture of the two. Without faith catastrophe will destroy us. Eigen says that faith is deeper than destruction, and destruction is deeper than faith; they are two parts of a dynamic. People feel there can be no faith after the Holocaust. Eigen says there is. Our faith is made more robust by the Holocaust, and yet the Holocaust preserves its awful magnitude. There is faith deeper than the Holocaust, yet the Holocaust is deeper than faith. It is just the way it is, he says. It is not one way; it is not the other. It is both.[6]

The value of seeing how opposites operate simultaneously as well as separately expands our experience and how we organize it. Eigen points out that our attitude often determines the extent to which we see the self-other and mind-body as distinct or united. Our attitudes are fluid—they can change: "We may be more mental or spiritual or physical at any given moment."[7]

The tiniest cell of experience is made of distinction-union tendencies that are "part of one structure or event, always mixed and working."[8] Even "emotional seas," obviously larger than a cell of experience, "move through our being, supporting and dashing it, blend into a vast unit that forms the background of our lives."[9]

Louise Gluck's poem "A Sharply Worded Silence" illustrates the back-and-forth movements, in this case from one mood to another:

> When I was young, she said, I liked walking the garden path at twilight. . . .
>
> I would see the moon rise.
>
> That was for me the great pleasure; not sex, not food, not worldly amusements.
>
> . . . But certain nights, she said, the moon was barely visible through the clouds . . .
>
> A night of pure discouragement.
>
> And still the next night I would begin again, and often all would be well.[10]

---

6. Eigen, online workshop.
7. Eigen, *Whirlwind*, xi.
8. Eigen, *Contact*, 1.
9. Ibid., 9.
10. Gluck, "Silence," 19.

PSYCHE, SOUL, AND SPIRIT

In Kabbalistic thought, some of the ten Sephirot—the attributes through which God reveals himself—are opposing forces. For example, God's attribute of kindness/compassion seems at odds with his attribute of justice/severity. Compassion taken too far might hinder a person from using his own resources to improve his condition. Justice can supply the necessary correction for compassion. But severity, taken too far, e.g., when one leaves others completely to their own devices, can be destructive. An example of severity tempered by compassion can be seen when spouses fight and they judge each other excessively. The impact of the attacks can be lessened by compassion for oneself and one's spouse, as Eigen points out. Compassion in this context enables us to wonder how we allowed ourselves to get carried away in this painful situation. Another example of mixing severity with compassion is embodied in the Zoroastrian prayer, "May the victory over the enemy be perfect, complete, and compassionate."

In the Jewish prayer (in Aramaic) "Introductory Prayer" it is said that God is the unity producing the ten Sephirot. When we connect and unite the Sephirot, we experience how God conducts the world. When one causes the ten Sephirot to diverge, one is regarded as if he has caused a divergence within God. Rabbi Pinhas of Koretz writes, "All the ten creative powers are contained in every single thing."[11] "Do not say, 'This is a stone and not God.' Rather, all existence is God, and the stone is a thing pervaded by divinity."[12] Rabbi Pinhas clearly sees the potential of each entity to merge with God. A person who is praying is wrong to think that his prayer is something apart from God; rather, "prayer in itself is God." In a story of a cobbler named Enoch, one sees how God pervades all work. When stitching sandals, Enoch whispers, "for the sake of uniting God and God's Shekhina."[13] (Shekinah is the dwelling of the divine presence of God.) In the same vein, Hasidism encourages letting the light "penetrate the darkness until the darkness itself shines and there is no longer any division between the two."[14]

The Pillar of Prayer, based on teachings from the Baal Shem Tov, centers around consciousness as a unifier of attributes that are separate but complementary. Human experience based on the Kabbalistic Tree of Life describes three pillars: one on the left, one on the right, and one in the center, which is consciousness as the unifier. Binah, on the left, represents

---

11. Buber, *Tales*, 1:122.
12. Matt, *Essential Kabbalah*, 24.
13. Magid, *Schachter-Shalomi*.
14. Buber, *Tales*, 2:59.

EXPLORING UNITY AND DISTINCTION

understanding, the root of creation, offering constant nurture and growth. Chokmah, on the right, represents wisdom, the root of the world of emanation, intuitive insight, a source of energy that puts things in motion. As the soul enters an awakened state, it moves back and forth between the left and right pillars. It is at home with sorrow, understanding, growth, destruction, and regeneration. It is also at home with joy, appreciation, insight, initiative, newness, and intuitive insight. Continuously touching base with the opposing pillars of depression and ecstasy, constriction and expansion, reflection and action, rest and play, the middle pillar keeps the ceiling from collapsing; it creates an arena of distinction-union, a place where opposites can blend and contrast.

Religion is concerned with permanence amid change and change amid permanence; the two complement each other. According to the philosopher A. N. Whitehead, the theme of cosmology, and the basis of all religions, is how the flux of this world's ephemera passes into everlasting unity. The idea is that God's vision "accomplishes its purpose of completion by absorption of the world's multiplicity of effort."[15]

Distinction-union can be seen in Whitehead's idea of God as having two natures. God's conceptual nature is distinct from his consequent nature, which is actual. His conceptual nature does not operate in a vacuum; it presupposes actuality and is united in the process of becoming one with every other creative act. In this it shares with individuals their deepest emotions, as "a fellow sufferer who understands."[16]

God also feels with us the awe and amazement that we experience before the forms of the natural world he created. By sharing our joy and amazement, he is an awestruck participant in the evolution of his creation. Eigen asks, "Doesn't Yosemite ignite God?" and continues, "the God I know wants to create, to taste the power that makes us giddy."[17] This idea is not a stranger to the Jewish prayers, in which God rejoices in his creation. That a concept presupposes actuality and consists of the power to create also appears in Kabbalah, where God's thinking of the good deeds of righteous men, not yet created, is enough to actualize the thought.[18]

---

15. Whitehead, *Process*, 411.
16. Ibid., 415.
17. Eigen, *Feeling*, 11–12.
18. Matt, *Essential Kabbalah*, 98.

PSYCHE, SOUL, AND SPIRIT

Whitehead sees God as "the perpetual vision of the road, which leads to deeper realities.... He is the ideal that sustains the world and binds it."[19] In Hasidic thought, binding the conceptual and the actual is our task. One feature of this binding is the suggestion that we not rebel against our desires but rather seize their power and bind them to God.[20] This is one of the revolutionary ideas of Hasidism, which does not reject obstacles to a spiritual life, but rather accepts and transforms them into aids for growth. Hasidism sees opposites such as prohibition and permission, guilt and innocence, as a unified whole. The philosopher Martin Buber points out that the Hasidic task is to transform the urge for evil into good in the midst of thousands of disappointments and obstacles. Moreover, the Hasid wants to retain the urge for evil, and to recover it when lost, as a tool for further transformation that will increase the good and get him closer to God.[21]

Another challenge is expressed in the Kabbalistic notion of kelipot (the husk of a kernel). These coverings came about at the time of creation, when vessels broke, unable to contain the holy light. The sparks from that light remained hidden in the shards. A person's lifelong task is to break open the kelipot and release the sparks—the Holy Essence hidden there. Indeed, our awareness and appreciation of God's light is the vessel that makes us evermore capable to receive his blessings.

This mystical notion gives rise to the question: to what extent are we able to receive and contain the light bestowed on us—goodness, gifts, and grace? Moreover, how often do we recognize these gifts, so that we can be grateful for them, and use them to our benefit and the benefit of others?

The longing for wholeness is evident in Rabbi Abraham Isaac Kook's mystical quest, which recognizes the unity between everything in the world—reason and imagination, theory and action. This follows from recognizing the unity of God. The quest also doesn't distinguish between great and small; it perceives all that exists as marked with value.[22] Rabbi Kook's view is life affirming, where nothing is invalid and nothing is lost—akin to Whitehead's idea that even evil is purified in God, and in God nothing is lost.

The psychoanalyst Franklin Sollars, in response to Eigen's ideas about the interplay of distinction and unity, writes, "I do like to think

---

19. Whitehead, *Religion*, 158.
20. Buber, *Tales*, 1:4.
21. Ibid., 1:4–5.
22. Kook, "Lights," 194.

EXPLORING UNITY AND DISTINCTION

there is a progression from distinction to union or a trope that tends towards consciousness expansion or unitive consciousness that transcends paradox. Maybe it's just the romantic in me but I like to think I am going somewhere. Progressing towards grace or nirvana or satori, which is beyond binaries and contradiction and even conflict. Somewhere, somehow, someday."[23]

Eigen profoundly respects Sollars's vision as a "good depiction of movement towards the better, the good, whole . . . that lifetime after lifetime we get better until there is no more evil." Eigen refers to the Lankavatara Sutra, which is similar to Sollars's point of view, but with an exception. It says, "We are there now, here and now, we are it this moment, in the place we are moving towards." The journey is now. Eigen also thinks of "the Catholic mystical schema: ordinary living, purgative stage, stage of mystical union with the Divine," and sees them as going on now. In a similar vein, in our own lives we feel a continual ebb and flow of evil and good, light and darkness. We move from living to dying and dying to living, from the sublime to the mundane, the ordinary to the divine. Eigen's vision embraces Buddha's transcendence and Christ's resurrection as "samsara-nirvana; crucifixion-resurrection, aspects of now states, tendencies, currents, moments, now."[24] Eigen, along with the psychoanalyst Wilfred Bion, sees fusion and splitting tendencies as simultaneous and oscillating—alternate ways of organizing experience.

The Pillar of Prayer expands on the concept of uniting with the divine. It talks of a mitzvah, a commandment by God, fulfilled with D'vekut, which is a cleaving with the divine that is so passionate that it contains within it all the mitzvoth. Another way of experiencing this unity is with Kavannah (intention), a state of mind in which one is fully absorbed and feels at one with what one is doing. The state of absorption supersedes words. If one is mainly aware of and united with the Presence of the Creator, then the darkness departs, a darkness that prevents the eyes from perceiving the Presence. In addition, the cleaving to the divine softens judgment and transforms it into divine compassion.

To be absorbed, to regenerate connection between oneself and God, one needs not to flinch from darkness or light, but rather to stay with it and keep looking at it. Kabbalah speaks of a spark of impenetrable darkness from which universes are born. Similarly, Eigen speaks of deep concentration,

23. Eigen, online workshop.
24. Ibid

looking at a point, when the more you look at it the more you see. A single point is a point of entry to universes. Eigen quotes the poet William Blake: "To see a World in a Grain of Sand / And a Heaven in a Wild Flower / Hold Infinity in the palm of your hand / And Eternity in an hour."[25]

The great saints of different religions are separated by their practices and beliefs; this separation allows each soul to grow into itself; but at the highest spiritual level they achieve a genuine spiritual unity. This is akin to the opposing ideologies that Rabbi Kook writes about. He stresses the need for the initial separation of each ideology so they grow and become distinct. He illustrates this with the need for an optimal separation between plants, so that each one has room to acquire their sustenance required for growth. He then writes that "even the dichotomies experienced will be unified through a higher enlightenment, which recognizes their aspect of unity and compatibility. In the content of man's life this is the entire basis for holiness."[26]

In Hasidism individuality as well as community are separate and conjoined. Hasidism talks about dichotomies but reveals a strong appreciation of unity through interaction between the zaddik (righteous one) and his disciples. Here a transmission of spirit occurs, dependent on soul resonance: the teacher serves as an example in whatever he does. He embodies the Torah as a living reality carrying the teachings in words and in silence. There are times when the disciple's manner of asking a question stirs the master and evokes his spirit.[27] There is a sense of comfort and encouragement that derives from this connection. Rabbi Yitzhak of Skvira tells of his grandfather Rabbi Nahum, who, when evaluating the state of his soul, thought he had sinned greatly, and was discouraged. But then, when thinking of his disciples' devotion to him, he felt that they would comfort him. When he saw them coming he envisioned two curved shapes fused into a ring.[28]

Like the rabbi who envisions himself linked to his disciple, Bion emphasizes the analyst and the analysand as two people linked together.[29] God as a fellow sufferer, the zaddik transmitting his spirit to his disciple; Bion's analysand who will not be satisfied unless he senses that the analyst experiences emotionally what *he* experiences—all of these speak to the significance of a relationship built on care and compassion.

25. Ibid.
26. Kook, "Lights," 225.
27. Buber, *Tales*, 1:8.
28. Ibid., 1:172–73.
29. Bion, *Cogitations*, 78.

EXPLORING UNITY AND DISTINCTION

In his books and in his analytical practice Eigen exhibits this quality of finding something in him that corresponds to what the analysand is going through. In a session with a patient, the patient said, "I'm stupid." Eigen replied, "I'm stupid too." This remark rippled. The patient felt that Eigen meant it, and she began not to feel stupid.

Although the Hasidic masters are above the fray in their wisdom and intuition, they make an effort not to distinguish themselves from their followers, to see and be seen as one of the people. Though they are highly revered (a crowded audience usually creates a path upon the arrival of their master), there is no sense of a hierarchy, of superiority and inferiority; rather, there is a sense of fellowship. Once at a parting, the Baal Shem blessed his disciple., then bowed his own head to receive the blessing from the disciple. The disciple was reluctant, but the Baal Shem took his hand and laid it on his own head.[30] Rabbi Bunum expands on that intimacy: as a man can only see his reflection in water when he bends close to it, "The heart of man must lean down to the heart of his fellow; then it will see itself within his heart."[31]

Rabbi Zusya also exemplifies the capacity to consider himself as one of the people, as equal to them. Zusya's loneliness, described by Buber, is that of one who identifies with others to the point of losing his own personhood: "His loneliness in the face of the eternal 'Thou' is not the loneliness of the recluse . . . but a loneliness which includes intrinsic oneness with all living creatures." (Is this the loneliness for the self that is lost?) Zusya regards the faults of his fellows as his own, "rejoicing in them [his fellows] and in all creatures in the freedom of God."[32]

Buber describes the zaddik Rabbi Nachman as having a deep sense of union with all "simple men." The author Chaim Potok, in his foreword to *Tales of the Hasidim*, tells of how Buber himself was disappointed with his retelling of the tales until he began to feel his "unity with the spirit of Rabbi Nachman. . . . I had found the true faithfulness: more adequately than the direct disciples, I received and completed the task, a later messenger in a foreign realm."[33]

The teachings of Kabbalah, Whitehead, and Eigen diverge from traditional dualistic thinking of good and evil. According to Eigen aspects of Kabbalah teach that the middle way is not just a balance—something

30. Buber, *Tales*, 1:100.
31. Ibid., 2:263.
32. Ibid., 1:27.
33. Ibid., 1:xiii–xiv.

new is created. This is the distinction-union that propels progression. Whitehead strikingly articulates this dynamic in his theory that opposing ideas are vital means of evolution. To Whitehead, creativity emerges from the reality that God and the World are opposites. The task of creativity is to transform disjointed multiplicity into unity, while diversities remain in contrast.[34] Whitehead's concept of contrasts as a basis for creative advance sees value in evil and destruction as forces that spur progress and growth.

Blake depicts the creative power of evil with even greater force. To him, opposites—love and hate, and even heaven and hell—cover only a limited existence when separated. However, when they struggle with each other something new is created. Unlike Kabbalah, Whitehead, and Eigen, who discuss opposites as reciprocal and reconciliatory, Blake stresses that opposites coexist and interact without reconciliation. He sees evil as giving birth to energy, which is not only necessary for existence but is synonymous with eternal delight. To Blake hell is not a punishment but rather a source of unrepressed energy for creativity. When desire is restrained it's because it's weakened by reason. In Blake's view, religion's attempt to "reconcile" reason and energy actually destroys existence. Blake's cover design for *The Marriage of Heaven and Hell* illustrates how the marriage will be consummated: Hell impregnates the passive and sterile Heaven, giving it life and energy.

Blake presents the idea of Infernal Wisdom. His "Proverbs of Hell" demonstrate the significance of individuality and living one's own life: "No bird soars too high, if he soars with his own wings."[35] This is a slam at the conventional religious idea that one must avoid hubris and not go beyond human limitations. Punishment was the lot of the people who attempted to build the tower of Babel, and of Prometheus, who stole the fire from heaven and gave it to people. But these are actions that Blake praises. Other proverbs are startling: "The road of excess leads to the palace of wisdom"[36] and "The tigers of wrath are wiser than the horses of instruction."[37] Blake seems to be saying that there can only be good where evil exists. Without evil, good is static and even deteriorates; destruction is a necessary element in construction. But without good, evil has nothing to destroy. According to him the opposition of good and evil is what holds existence together. He says to his "friend" the angel: "Opposition is true friendship" because it is the only thing

---

34. Whitehead, *Process*, 410.
35. Blake, *Marriage*, xviii.
36. Ibid.
37. Ibid., xix.

EXPLORING UNITY AND DISTINCTION

with transformative power; there is no harmony of positive and negative forces; the two must remain separate in order to interact productively.[38]

Buber's notion of I and Thou is another example of distinction-union. Potok describes how Buber thought that the early Hasidic community embodied I and Thou: man to man and man to God as relation, not subject-object, not I and it, user to used. Buber saw this relation as "sacred betweenness."[39] Craig Gilliam reads Buber as saying that when there is an authentic encounter between I and the other, our humanness and the humanness of the other meet. What then arises is the divine: "The in-between where two meet is where God or the divine happens."[40]

Eigen explores a similar phenomenon, the self intersecting with the other: "Oceanic fusion, absorption, or oneness would not do justice to the drama. . . . For one thing, the mystical moment may involve enormous upheaval, turbulence, over-throwing and reworking of self. A new meeting can change one's picture of what self and other can be."[41]

Bion uses the word *sacred* to imply a space deserving reverence. His context is different from Buber's. Bion, a psychoanalyst, recommends that the therapist enter a session clear of memory, desire, understanding, and expectation. This space gives room for intuition and for mystical experience. In Bion's theory, analyst and patient become or approximate becoming. They transcend separateness by evolving and transforming in that space. The interaction of therapist and patient, or indeed the interaction of any subject and object, and all opposites, creates something greater than either opposite provides. In this case it is not the gray area between black and white, but instead something more vivid than either.

The psychoanalyst D. W. Winnicott used the term *transitional phenomenon* to describe a space between the child merging with mother and the child being separated from her. According to Eigen this opens up an idea that also includes experiences such as between writer and reader. Eigen feels that transitional experiencing is continuous throughout Winnicott's work and is similar to how a literary metaphor opens up something new about the object it describes. Only a relationship between the two terms can achieve this novelty. The impact that each separate thing makes when connected is greater than when separated, and the deeper sense of both are guaranteed.

38. Ibid., xv.
39. Buber, *Tales*, 1:xii.
40. Gilliam, "Half-Fast Walk."
41. Eigen, *Mystic*, 31.

PSYCHE, SOUL, AND SPIRIT

Unity with his disciples for a zaddik can effect change and transformation in him and in the world. As described above, a vision of unity among Hasidim changed one zaddik's emotions from feeling dispirited to feeling encouraged. The zaddik alone cannot achieve what a gathering of individuals can achieve praying or rejoicing. The Baal Shem tells of how once after the Day of Atonement the new moon did not appear from behind the clouds. The joy of the Hasidim brought about the appearance of the moon so that the blessing of the new moon could be made. A zaddik, even one with a powerful soul, could not achieve that.[42] Similarly, the Sh'ma prayer recited in the synagogue together exceeds the power of Sh'ma recited individually.

Another source for transformation into wholeness and unity with others is expressed in *The Palm Tree of Devorah*, in which Cordovero says that acquiring the attribute of Binah (understanding) is achieved by returning to God in full repentance. A person who spends all of his days in repentance, immersing himself in it, will find his evil tendencies corrected. That which he experiences as severe is sweetened. With this level of understanding evil deeds "enter the higher worlds and become rooted in holiness there, transforming themselves into good rather than becoming nullified."[43] Even Cain could have transformed had he only repented.

To St. Bonaventure union and love are connected. He describes love as transformatory, simply because love unites. While the union exists one is "forced to conform in action with the object" of one's love. This does not mean that the lover is transformed into the beloved himself, but that he is united with the beloved and that he will conform—be like him—in his actions.[44] Bonaventure also says that while love contacts, knowledge abstracts. Interestingly, however, having sexual intercourse in the Bible is referred to as "knowing."

Geographically and in terms of a way of life and outlook, Ralph Waldo Emerson could not be further away from Hasidism, and yet a thread runs between him and Hasidic thought. In his essay "The Over-Soul" Emerson writes of that common heart, the soul of the whole, "to which every part and particle is equally related; the eternal ONE. . . . We see the world piece by piece, as the sun, the moon, the animal the tree; but the whole, of which these are the shining parts, is the soul."[45] His thinking is similar to Ha-

---

42. Buber, *Tales*, 1:8.
43. Cordovero, *Palm Tree*, 80.
44. Prentice, *Bonaventure*, 72–73.
45. Emerson, *Complete Essays*, 262.

sidic thought, which sees and appreciates unity in manifold places—within oneself, among others, and with the divine. He sees heart as the heart of all, as "one blood that rolls uninterruptedly through all men, as the water of the globe is all one sea."[46] And like Hasidic thought, which sees God, the divine, irrigating the Tree of Life through a spring that is likened to the soul giving life to the body, and sees the zaddik linking with others and the divine as a way of transformation, Emerson reveres the soul that will no longer weave a life of shreds and patches, but will live in a divine unity.

While Emerson stresses a deep connection between all men, Winnicott, in one of his papers, focuses on how in even the most intimate contact we still maintain lack of contact, even total isolation: "At the center of each person is an incommunicado element, and this is sacred and most worthy of preservation", because of a feeling of "threat to the isolated core, the threat of being found, altered."[47]

A completely different context that presents us with a sense of lack of contact may be seen in St. John of the Cross's arid periods—the dark night of the soul—together with his attempts to reach God. Rebbe Nachman at times feels close to God and at other times decries God for not listening to him for a long time, for being distant and unreachable.[48] Eigen talks about patients in a similar vein: "Patients are radically threatened . . . and confused by how near and far they feel to themselves and others. This distance-closeness is not something that is 'curable.'"[49]

Moreover, according to Eigen there are times in therapeutic sessions when the patient needs to build a tolerance for blankness and lack of distinctions. "The moment's rest between surges of mental content might come to be valued as an opening in being." If the therapist is silent the silence can serve as a methodology for the patient to build his tolerance and learn the value of "waiting and identifying with the dark, blank horizon."[50]

The opening that Eigen often talks about can take many forms, and can be seen in different contexts. Here is one in which the poet Rainer Maria Rilke writes about the ripening of an individual to love and unity:

> Loving does not at first mean merging, surrendering, and uniting
> with another person (for what would a union be of two people

---

46. Ibid., 276.
47. Winnicott, "On Communication," 185.
48. Kallus, *Pillar of Prayer*, 59.
49. Eigen, *Psychotic Core*, 311.
50. Ibid., 307–8.

PSYCHE, SOUL, AND SPIRIT

who are unclarified, unfinished, and still incoherent?), it is a high inducement for the individual to ripen, to become something in himself, to become world, to become world in himself for the sake of another person; it is a great, demanding claim on him, something that chooses him and calls him to vast distances. Only in this sense, as the task of working on themselves ("to hearken and to hammer day and night"), may young people use the love that is given to them. Merging and surrendering and every kind of communion is not for them (who must still, for a long, long time, save and gather themselves); it is the ultimate, is perhaps that for which human lives are as yet barely large enough.[51]

---

51. Rilke, "Letter 7," 69–70.

2

ST. TERESA OF AVILA: ENDURING SUFFERING FOR ONE'S VALUES

IN HER AUTOBIOGRAPHY, ST. Teresa of Avila writes of her spiritual journey, describing her experiences—especially her difficulties and her suffering—and exhibiting endurance in regard to them and to internal and external attacks for implementing her values. She relates her troubles in detail. Being completely honest, she neither dramatizes nor downplays their importance, telling it the way it is. This makes for a great gift to all. And she means to help. She wants the reader to benefit from her experiences. St. Teresa herself learned by experience: "I could have learned little from books, for until His majesty taught it to me by experience what I learned was nothing at all."[1]

Teresa is probably more known for her remarkable contemplative life, but she was equally gifted in her active religious life, integrating the two. She founded seventeen Carmelite convents and monasteries for the purpose of reforming the practices that had become lax in observance of the rules of enclosure and the vows of poverty. She was adept at persuasion. On one occasion she was able to convince the Father General, who had been sent from Rome, to grant permission to found enclosed monasteries for friars by explaining why it would be in service to God and also a great service to "Our Lady," knowing that the General was extremely devoted to the Virgin Mary, the mother of Jesus. Note how Teresa zeroes in on the Father General's preference. In her real estate dealings (to find suitable houses) she could hold her own with well-born ladies, and was able to get the aid of the king himself. She could also converse casually with villagers about market prices and the progress of crops; she became popular with common people as well as with the aristocracy. While on her journeys to found the reformed religious houses, Teresa went through great physical hardships, but she faced them with courage and encouraged her assistants to follow suit. In the carriages

---

1. Teresa, *Complete Works*, 137.

on these journeys she would entertain with poems she made up on the spot, and she engaged everyone in spirited conversations. She was very mindful not to neglect the religious duties of her group. She was also able to stop the rancor of the other travelers by conversing about God. She took care to provide food and shelter for her people in the most primitive inns. Having founded a convent, she would stay until it was clean, provided with necessities, and arranged just so—until it was a going concern.

Teresa's contemplative life developed gradually. Even as a very young child she wanted to be a martyr so that she could go to heaven. However, as a teenager, by her own account, she indulged in gossiping and other vanities with a relative whom the family considered a bad influence and from whom, Teresa says, she learned about all kinds of evil. Teresa does not specify the evil (nor the vanities), yet it was such that the family removed her from the home and sent her to board at a convent to be brought back to virtue. At this convent Teresa was very popular: "All the nuns were pleased with me; for the Lord had given me grace, wherever I was, to please people, and so I became a great favorite."[2] Teresa returned to her love for spiritual things and removed some of her aversion to being a nun. But she became seriously ill and returned to her father's house.

Conversations with a devout uncle led Teresa to understand what she had learned as a child: "that all things are nothing, and that the world is vanity and will soon pass away."[3] She thought if she had died of her illness she would have gone to hell. She weighed the suffering of being a nun against that of purgatory and hell, and forced herself to enter the religious life. Her motivation to become a nun, by her own admission, was a poor one—servile fear, not love.

When Teresa told her father of her desire to enter a convent, he withheld his consent. The most he gave was permission to do as she liked after his death. According to her the devil attacked her the minute she determined to be a nun, suggesting to her that she had been too delicately brought up to endure the trials of religious life. Teresa's conflict lasted for three months. She fought against herself but received courage from God to make the decision to enter the convent. She was in poor health for a year, with fainting fits, heart trouble, and other ailments. She attributes this to the change in her life and to the change in diet, but does not elaborate.

2. Ibid., 16.
3. Ibid., 18.

ST. TERESA OF AVILA

We do know that she was not prepared for the grief and fear involved in abandoning her intense relationships with friends and family.

The convent Teresa enters is the sphere of her spiritual trials; frivolous conversations, gossip, and vanities keep her from God and are good reasons for her to rebuke herself for indulging in them. For a while, she feels unworthy to pray because of her indulgences. (In fact, she spends her first eighteen years in the convent in a conflict about being engaged with worldly pleasures while in the convent.) As she evolves she experiences great favors and consolations from God when in states of prayer and contemplation. She describes how in the fourth degree of prayer—the prayer of union with God and the elevation that takes place in that union—there is "only rejoicing, unaccompanied by any understanding of the thing in which the soul is rejoicing."[4] She searches for words great enough to characterize the experience: "the greatest blessing which may be possessed upon earth," "sublimity," "bliss," "sweet delight." She reports that sometimes the soul "issues from itself, like a fire that is burning and has become wholly flame,"[5] noting that God began not only to give them but to be pleased that others should know that he was giving them to her. When fellow nuns and spiritual directors learn about her experiences they have a good opinion of her. "Then suddenly began evil-speaking and persecution. . . . They said that I wanted to become a saint, and that I was inventing new-fangled practices though in many respects I had not even achieved the full observance of my Rule, nor had I attained to the goodness and sanctity of nuns in my own house."[6] They also accuse her of being deceived by the devil, for surely they think God would not reward someone who by her own admission is a sinner. This is the beginning of the opposition that Teresa encounters throughout her life.

Teresa doesn't deny the fact that she hasn't followed the discipline fully; in fact she uses the accusations as a spur to examine herself for faults. For example, she realizes that telling people about her weaknesses is not out of humility, but is a way of deflecting attacks on her for receiving favors from God. When she was a beginner she didn't know that God's plan for her included sweetness and pleasure, not just suffering—that God rewards us in this lifetime with feelings that are generally associated with the devil. She advances from feeling discomfort about receiving God's grace to complete

---

4. Ibid., 105.
5. Ibid., 106.
6. Ibid., 115.

acceptance of the grace and its consequences. She knows that to be bestowed with grace has nothing to do with her will—it is his will. She insists that grace have its proper place: "We may think it humility not to realize that the Lord is bestowing gifts upon us. Let us understand very, very, clearly, how this matter stands. God gives us these gifts for no merit of ours."[7]

The resolution of Teresa's conflict in regard to grace and divine favors stirs us to contemplate how often we close ourselves to grace—sometimes in order to placate the opposition—and it motivates us to face our predicament regarding our own spirituality: if we do what the world values and neglect our spirit, we will suffer; if we remain consonant with our spirit and let it flourish, the world will attack us and we will still suffer, but for our own values. Teresa's conflict opens our eyes to our own guilt when we feel more fortunate than others and to our fear of attacks. It is helpful to remember that Teresa needs more courage to receive favors from God than to endure her worst suffering.

On one occasion Teresa has a vision while in prayer: she sees herself all alone in a great field, completely surrounded by people carrying lances, swords, daggers, and rapiers for the purpose of attacking her. Soon Teresa realizes that the vision is a picture of the world. She knows that these people—friends, relatives, and "what amazes me the most, very good people"[8]—attack her soul, motivated by worldliness. They attack her because she shuns attention, honor, and fame, preferring to follow what she loves and what she values and to be in affinity with God rather than follow the world and be accepted or admired by it. She recognizes, unabashedly, that "a soul which God allows to walk in this way in the sight of the whole world may well prepare itself to be martyred by the world, for, if it will not die to the world of its own free will, the world itself will kill it."[9] Each encounter with worldly values, whether in the secular world or among religious people, reinforces Teresa's disdain for worldliness, and she gradually learns to put her trust more fully in her knowledge of what God wants her to do, withdrawing her attention from the opinions of people.

The attacks on Teresa also have all the earmarks of destructive envy and the desire to cut down a truly superior person. The envy is understandable, not only for God's favors to her—visions, locutions, and raptures—but also, maybe especially, for the freedom she has to be herself and for her

---

7. Ibid., 59.
8. Ibid., 287.
9. Ibid., 210.

individual way of relating to God. Though there is no evidence that she reports her conversations with God to the other nuns, they must sense her capacity to be intimate with God. Teresa approaches God as a fellow human being—sometimes as a friend or a lover, sometimes as her boss for whom she is doing all this work, claiming the right to be helped by him, expecting him to live up to his word and help her. She is bold enough to pressure God: "I believe I told Him then that I would not rise from that spot until He had granted me what I was beseeching of Him."[10] She reproaches God for hiding from her and wonders how this is consistent with his mercy, and she chides him, saying it is no wonder he has so few friends considering the way he treats them. She complains that if she were able to hide from him he would not be able to endure it.

At times Teresa views mental prayer as simply a conversation between friends. She is open to hear God's advice, often spoken in a direct and conversational tone, on the most mundane and the most sublime issues. When she wonders what to write concerning the foundation of a particular convent, the Lord asks her, what more does she want "than to realize that its foundation had been miraculous?"[11] When some people advise her not to let anyone who was not well-born be buried in her convent, she hears the Lord dismissively say, "Thou wilt act very foolishly, daughter, if thou regardest the laws of the world."[12] On a sublime note, Teresa recalls her vision of the Lord who appears to her after having communicated, "comforting me with great consolations, taking her hands and putting them to his side, saying, 'See My wounds. Thou art not without Me. Life is short and soon passes.'"[13] This example of Teresa's "great consolations" is not a ready-made, churchly formula; it is idiosyncratically hers.

The great comfort provided by Teresa's visions and locutions—her contacts with God—more than make up for her suffering. One time she sees "a complete representation of this most sacred Humanity [a vision of Jesus], just as in a picture of His resurrection body, in very great beauty and majesty."[14] She describes the effects of such visions: "there is such a beauty about glorified bodies that the glory which illumines them throws all who

10. Ibid., 54.
11. Ibid., 339.
12. Ibid., 338.
13. Ibid., 341.
14. Ibid., 179.

PSYCHE, SOUL, AND SPIRIT

look upon such supernatural loveliness into confusion."[15] One of Teresa's confessors wrote that without her visions she could not have endured "such an inestimable amount of trouble, opposition and illness as she has had to bear, and has to bear still, for she is never without some kind of suffering."[16]

Teresa's locutions sometimes give her spiritual direction in a practical way. Once, when wondering why the "more faithful" nuns should not be given the graces and favors God bestows on her, she hears the Lord say, "Serve thou Me, and meddle not with this."[17] When thinking about the mistakes she makes in business matters in founding the convents, and how she cannot remain pure, she hears, "There is no help for that, daughter. Strive thou always to have a right intention and to be detached in everything, and look to Me."[18] She writes that when she told God that her confessor told her to stop praying, fearing that the devil was responding to her prayers, "He seemed to me to have become angry, and He told me to tell them that this was tyranny."[19] Sometimes the locutions are on a more elevated plane. When in a rapture, she hears, "I will have thee converse now, not with men, but with angels."[20] In that moment she is free to give up her friendships, which she has struggled without success to relinquish.

Teresa's visions and locutions eventually help her detach from the opinions of people and rely only on God and Jesus as true companions. Through her relationship with God, the strengthening she receives from the visions and locutions, she can overcome attacks: "out of a zeal for righteousness, people may speak very ill of me, and others are afraid to have anything to do with me or to hear my confessions, while still others say all kinds of things to my face, I care about it—Glory be to God—very little."[21] Over the years her love of solitude increases. She feels that if she were to leave all her friends and relatives (the latter tire her anyway) it would amount to very little. By focusing on her service to God she perseveres through neutralizing rather than tackling the opposition.

The persecutions confirm Teresa's way of perfection. Who would bother to persecute her if she weren't striving to do God's will, to strip herself of

15. Ibid.
16. Ibid., 325.
17. Ibid., 115.
18. Ibid., 339.
19. Ibid., 189.
20. Ibid., 155.
21. Ibid., 297.

worldly desire? The attacks are particularly fierce when she founds her first new convent, St. Joseph's in Avila. The purpose of the convent is to protect and enhance the contemplative life, eliminating anything that interferes with that. "This will always be the aim of our nuns—to be alone with Him only."[22] When Teresa's plans for the convent become known, she is attacked, and she reports the attack in a matter-of-fact way: "People talked about us, laughed at us and declared that the idea was ridiculous."[23] They thought it was the ridiculous idea of some women. The nuns in her own convent resent her desire to build a new convent; they say she is insulting them, as they believe the money should instead go to their convent. Some say she should be thrown into a prison cell in the convent. The provincial first approves of the plan but, fearing the opposition, later reneges; a friend who is helping her is refused absolution unless she gives up the idea of the project. Opposition is not only fierce but also vicious. Teresa's plans for her convent constitute an implied criticism of the existing convents and monasteries; perhaps this is what provokes such a counterattack, since every value has an opposing value. By this time, however, Teresa is so sure this is what God wants her to do that nothing, not even warnings by people close to her about having to appear before the Inquisition, deters her from continuing with her project or diminishes her conviction.

Teresa's self-confidence, however, is met with self-doubt. Only three or four hours after the convent is opened, the devil makes her wonder whether she has made a mistake and whether she has been disobedient in not getting a sanction from the provincial. She doubts that people could be contented under the new strict rule, whether "the whole thing was not ridiculous."[24] (She identifies with the aggressor, to the point of using the same derogatory word, *ridiculous*, against herself.) In other words, she doubts the value of the entire enterprise, undermining all that her better self knows. "All that the Lord had commanded me, all the opinions I had been seeking and the prayers I had been saying almost continuously for over two years—all these things fled from my memory as if they had never existed. . . . I had not the power to turn any of them [the virtues] into practice or defend myself against all these blows . . . my anguish was like a death agony."[25]

---

22. Ibid., 260.
23. Ibid., 221.
24. Ibid., 251.
25. Ibid.

PSYCHE, SOUL, AND SPIRIT

How helpful is this life-size saint when we relate her experiences to the level of our own quests, our explorations of new territories. Just plan to take a step forward in your career or personal relationships, and what devilish voices you'll hear inside your head: "Who are you to think you can do that?" "Are you sure you want to work so hard?" "Be careful; if you have such high standards, you'll be left alone!" On the other hand, we know when a good idea is good; we can hear the voice of our unconscious telling us, "This is good. Do it." Following Teresa's example, we can trust the voice and resist the temptation to abandon a plan. At a point when suddenly the venture doesn't make sense to us, we can go back to our first impulse, when the thing made sense, and give it life.

It is hard to accept the fact of opposition to our doing something good. Most of us want people to be more well wishing than they are. This desire is costly, often leading to hurt and disappointment. Implied in Teresa's statement is the advice that we need to anticipate attacks from people when we venture on a new idea or project, especially if we openly and successfully refuse to conform to the current culture, and revolt against it—in fact asking for a counterattack. When one lives from one's true self, objections abound—without and within. Teresa is keenly aware of the price she pays for single-mindedly following God and her goal of being with God, but she knows she is strengthened, her courage increased by God, when she pays the price. One of her confessors wrote, "In the persecutions she had to bear, which were numerous, she found comfort, and she had a particular love for her persecutors."[26]

Teresa's attacks by the devil, like our own, are tailored to her weaknesses—her fear that she lacks humility (pride vs. humility is a big issue for her) and her knowledge of her delicate health. Subsequently she learns not to pay attention to her health and need for rest, so as not to invite the devil to attack. We make ourselves vulnerable to the devil, she says, by contracting attachments, for example, to honors, possessions, and pleasures, rather than to serving God. We could add examples of our own: attachments such as to being liked, to name and fame, and to our good reputation, which prevent us from implementing what we value. "By loving and desiring what we ought to hate," she says, "we become our own enemies—and they will do us much harm."[27] She relates that sometimes the devil sends pleasures when the soul is in deep prayer, but if the soul is humble, not eager for even

26. Ibid., 324.
27. Ibid., 165.

spiritual delights, and is devoted to helping Jesus bear his cross, the devil is thwarted. Another way to frustrate the devil is by confrontation. She challenges her devils: "'Come on, now, all of you,' I said: 'I am a servant of the Lord and I want to see what you can do to me.'"[28] Teresa unflinchingly faces the fact of evil and presents methods for counterattack.

The suffering Teresa experiences in terms of opposition and self-doubt is compounded by fear. We may think that Teresa, like us, would deplore her fear. (She does in fact distinguish between servile fear—a low-level fear—and fear about falling short of her goals and about whether she deserves the favors she receives from God.) She is aware of the pitfalls of fear: "It is of great importance, when we begin to practice prayer, not to let ourselves be frightened by our own thoughts."[29] She advises the reader not to let fear be a deterrent when one is sure that the plan is not a whim but comes from God. Though Teresa is tortured by her fear, she is able to step back and see it as a test of her conviction, a need to confirm that indeed she is committed. To Teresa fear has a positive value, and she goes so far as to say that God is leading her by the road of fear. Fear is not a sign that she should stop doing what she is doing; rather it tells her not to be afraid that "things will turn out amiss, since He is all-powerful."[30]

Teresa becomes adept at seeing God in the midst of her tortures, in finding meaning in her terror, in realizing that something significant is going on, something supernatural, beyond understanding. The trials Teresa suffers connect her more to God. There are times when a few simple words from God, such as "Be not troubled; have no fear," provide her with relief, helping her see there is nothing wrong with her. She is then able to rejoice in God, wondering how he allows her to suffer such tortures but telling him that when these tortures are over she receives numerous favors. "My soul seemed to emerge from the crucible like gold, both brighter and purer, to find the Lord within it."[31] The rewards from God that ensue are in proportion to the fear.

As Teresa makes progress in her spiritual growth, she is inclined to value her suffering more and more: "though He would let me suffer a little, He would comfort me in such a way that it is nothing to me to desire trials.

---

28. Ibid., 164.
29. Ibid., 76.
30. Ibid., 21.
31. Ibid., 200.

... To die, Lord, or to suffer! I ask nothing else of Thee for myself but this."[32] How many people can relate to her plea for suffering? Some of us, however, do know from experience that when we recover from suffering there is a strong sense of well-being, a change in perspective, and a longing to live from the true self.

Teresa's capacity to be open to God, to be open to whatever comes, helps her be comforted. She describes how she felt once when she was not able to recollect herself: she was "restless and upset . . . battling and striving. . . . I was afraid, seeing how wicked I was that the favors which the Lord had granted me might be illusions."[33] She then experiences the Lord telling her not to think herself forgotten, for he would never leave her. Often, she says, he says to her, "Now thou art Mine and I am thine."[34] Her suffering is a vehicle for intimate connectedness.

Teresa is deeply aware of her experiences of joy and sorrow—joy in raptures and in God comforting her; sorrow when a good companion leaves. She feels the anguish when distant from God; she agonizes over her faults. She has become so sensitive and so in tune with how she experiences herself that she is able to notice her conscience switching almost instantaneously from being benign to being strict, and vice versa. We relate to how her strict conscience spoils the comfort she receives from God, and can imagine the relief she feels when her strict conscience turns benign. Teresa's experiences are everything to her. She remembers them, she refers to them, she learns from them. We identify with her! Those of us who work on discovering ourselves and who are open to being inspired by her draw example and permission to attend to our feelings as we experience them—the positive and the negative.

Teresa sees that people think it's a good thing to follow the pleasures and vanities of the world and speak ill of those who devote themselves to God. This creates a need in the spiritual person to seek the companionship of others, until the person "is strong enough not to be depressed by suffering."[35] She longs to companion Jesus in his suffering, perhaps partly because of her need for companionship and her understanding of how vital it is to spiritual growth and well-being; in addition, some of her best and most comforting moments are when companioned by him. Her need

---

32. Ibid., 297.
33. Ibid., 287.
34. Ibid.
35. Ibid., 47.

remains, however, for a contemporary companion, someone who understands and confirms her experiences because of his own experiences, someone who knows her suffering by acquaintance. But that does not come easily. An early confessor, although a holy man according to Teresa, does not trust his own opinion and succumbs to the slander about her. Many people believe—this is the worst of her trials—that, deceived by the devil as a result of her sins, she imagines her visions. She attempts to convince these people that her spiritual growth could only come from her contacts with God, but to no avail. In Fray Peter of Alcantara she finds the companionship she seeks. He validates her experiences and confirms that the opposition of good people is one of the most severe trials in the world. He commends her to her confessor, with the goal of looking with a positive eye at her experience.

Neither human companions nor Jesus, however, can provide a remedy for Teresa's great extremity of loneliness, which grows in proportion to her desire to get closer to God: "The soul soars upwards . . . and God causes it to be so completely bereft of everything that . . . it can find nothing on earth to bear it company. Nor does it desire company; it would rather die in its solitude."[36] This loneliness is from God, a means to show her soul that it is far away from God.

As she progresses in spirituality, Teresa's fears "evolve" also. Fears about whether her visions and locutions come from God or from the devil plague her. Although comforted by the assurance of Fray Peter of Alcantara that she is not being deceived by the devil, for a while she has insufficient trust in him to relinquish her fears and continues to believe for a long time the people (among them spiritual leaders) who tell her that her visions come from the devil. She is afraid that the delight and sweetness she feels in her prayers come from the devil, yet she knows in a deeper part of herself that these consolations are from God. We see Teresa not resting until, having absorbed her experiences in all their nuances, she is able to discern that her visions indeed come from God; her soul knows that the tranquility and benefits she experiences after having her visions could not but be from God.

Teresa tells the reader what are some of the other distinguishing marks of the work of God in the Prayer of Quiet. If a vision is from God there is a speedy rise from falling; for example, there is no need to look for ways to have humility because God will reveal to us the light of humility. Our own "puny reflections," she says, are nothing compared to the light that comes

---

36. Ibid., 122.

from God. God imparts this light to teach us that "we ourselves have nothing good," and "the greater are the favors we receive from Him, the better we learn it." Knowing this, we put ourselves in his hands and "we experience a security combined with humility and fear with respect to our salvation."[37] This fear is mature; it issues from faith. On the other hand, if the state of quiet comes from the devil, "it leaves neither light in the understanding nor steadfastness in the will."[38] Locutions from the devil not only fail to leave good effects but leave bad ones—aridity, disquiet, bewilderment, discontent. The humility that results is false; it is devoid of tranquility. We are provided with criteria for distinguishing true and constructive voices from false destructive advice, which has the aim of blocking or destroying creativity. Applying the concept of mature fear to our own life, we learn to dread not being what we could be.

The unpretentiousness of Teresa's personality, both her greatness and her ordinariness as they come across through the immediacy of her writings, enables the reader to apply her outlook, understanding, and actions to his or her daily life. Though she is a great saint, she is not a natural saint as was St. John of the Cross; she has to work at being one.

Longing to bear her suffering with the utmost detachment, constantly finding fault with her forbearance, she seeks ways to live with God, to be open to God, and to keep her eye on life with God after death. When she acts from her conviction she exhibits great strength, yet she is often beset by fears and severe self-doubt. Among those glorious days of being integrated, feeling at one with herself and with God and being detached from worldliness, Teresa still has days, and periods of several days at a time, in which good thoughts, visions, and the courage to be virtuous leave her. She has bodily pains, she cannot think of God, she is unable to think one good thought, and her faults loom large. On those days she feels that she will not be able to resist the temptations or slanders of the world, that her desire for solitude is not strength but weakness, and that she is no longer detached from people who oppose her.

We are moved by Teresa's trials, her struggle to discern between visions and locutions of God and those of the devil, her distress mingled with joy in regard to the favors received from God, and her torments in regard to her encounters with confessors, fellow nuns, and advisors. We feel relief

---

37. Ibid., 95.
38. Ibid., 93.

when Fray Peter comes on the scene. Teresa's need for companionship is itself companioning to us; even this great saint had this human need.

She is an example of allowing no obstacle, least of all her fears, to stop her from pursuing excellence and achieving her goal. She has the talent and capacity to utilize her suffering in the service of her goals: to devote herself single-mindedly to God and to enable others to do the same. Her fears alert her to the need to reflect, to assess her progress, to challenge herself, and to consolidate her powers in the service of new undertakings. Teresa's acceptance and endurance of her suffering strengthens her. Her courage in working with her suffering, in turn, strengthens us.

3

BEING AND THE SELF: I AM, BUT WHO AM I?

The essence of a person has captured the imagination of religious and psychoanalytic thinkers. What is real in us? How deep is it? How do we reach it? There's a human longing to reach that place, to decipher it, to live from it, to see how, if we touch it, it can improve our lives by opening possibilities for creative living. Impossible to locate, it is akin to what the psychoanalyst Michael Eigen once remarked as to whether you can talk about consciousness as you do when you pick a flower and say, "I have it."

The psychoanalyst D. W. Winnicott, in deciphering the workings of the self to support what is real in the person, sometimes uses the words *true self, core, central self,* and *center of gravity* as corresponding terms. However, at one point he characterizes the true self as a kind of organ that expresses itself in living. At times he uses *core* and sometimes *true self* to indicate the isolated kernel of the self. It seems that the true self and the core both communicate and don't communicate, depending on context. In 1963, however, Winnicott said, "I am putting forward and stressing the importance of the idea of the permanent isolation of the individual and claiming that at the core of the individual there is no communication with the not-me world."[1]

In the beginning, according to Winnicott, the baby is in a state of absolute dependence on the mother, and she must be in the state of maternal preoccupation for the center of gravity to be felt. The mother doesn't have to do anything or be anybody but herself, a source of nourishment, and if she *is* the baby also can *be*. Thus she provides a protective environment free of impingements that insures that the baby *is*, relaxing and enjoying in a state of unintegration.

This process can carry on throughout adult life where the individual protects his/her trueness from outside influence. If at any new beginning as adults we protect ourselves from external stressors, not reacting to external

---

1. Winnicott, "Communicating," 189–90.

impingements, being relaxed, we can emerge as creative, truly alive. It is akin to the state of purposeless playing, which starts in infancy and may recur in adult life if one has retained the capacity for unintegration.

Winnicott sees being as a necessary stage for living creatively and for creative work. He summarizes his paper on creativity and its origins thus: "After being—doing and being done to. But first, being."[2] Being is the foundation of self-discovery and creativity. If doing is not preceded by being—"I am"—the doing has no meaning for the doer and the doer does not feel real while doing. But too often we succumb to the temptation to do as a way of participating in life and being productive, to be this or that, in order to feel we exist, leaving out being and losing the source of vitality for doing and for becoming in the sense of evolving.

To discover the self one needs a reliable figure, a supportive presence or a benign psychic presence. This presence can be mother, God, or any other human or divine figure that one trusts; for trust is at the essence of the discovery of self. With a trusted person, according to Winnicott, "the individual can come together and exist as a unit, not as a defence against anxiety but as an expression of I Am, I am alive, I am myself. From this position everything is creative."[3]

Interestingly, according to Eigen there is an overlap of his idea of faith with Winnicott's idea of trust: a faith or trust that facilitates an opening to something unknown. Trust or faith allows for opening up and being receptive to possibility; it allows for unrelated thoughts to emerge, for free association, and ultimately for a novel experience. A new insight emerges for the Buddhist saint Milarepa when attacked by demons: having faith in his Guru Marpa, he calls on him for help, and then he remembers that the demons are his own, recalled only with the aid of the benign psychic presence of his guru.

Winnicott's notion of the true self, the source of what we experience as real, issues in a personal idea that is our own—a creative idea, a spontaneous gesture that is not learned or repeated but emerges from something true to us. This true self is enriched through its expressing itself in the world, through living in the world. If you hide the true self continuously to protect it, it not only won't grow but also will atrophy. "We cannot reach this true self through insight or introspection. Only by living from this authorizing

---

2. Winnicott, *Playing*, 85.
3. Ibid., 56.

idiom do we know something of that person sample that we are."[4] To Eigen the true self is too narrow a concept. He sees how the true self could be tyrannical in certain contexts, and he is wary of our inner tyrants, persecutors, and severe watchmen, our inner one-eyed monsters, which watch and torment us. We are caretakers of our inner life, as St. Teresa of Avila monstrated. She talks about the soul as being a garden and the need to cultivate it and water it—attend to it.

To the philosopher A. N. Whitehead, being and becoming cannot be separated. Being is constituted by the dynamism of becoming, which indicates that being is dynamic. Being arises "due to becoming." The basis of Whitehead's entire metaphysics is process, and he addresses being in terms of process—the becoming of experience. Everything continuously changes and moves on, while at the same time maintaining temporarily permanent aspects of reality. The dynamism of becoming results in processes that interact with each other; for example, moving from science to poetry or from biology to spirituality. In the case of Winnicott, when doing comes out of being it expresses the true self as it becomes.

There is a religious sensibility in the works of both Winnicott and Whitehead. If we think of Winnicott's notions of being as a foundation of aliveness and of the baby having a center of gravity, we could be led to the idea of God as a support. Another example of religious sensibility is Winnicott's idea that a person's central incommunicado element is sacred and in need of being preserved: "The violation of the self's core, the alteration of the self's central elements by communication seeping through the defences . . . would be the sin against the self."[5] As to Whitehead, the idea of God is refulgent in his entire philosophy of process. His God has a dual nature, a combination of permanence and change, evolving with the world. One side of his "primordial/conceptual nature" is his being, which has no actuality. It is infinite, eternal, free, deficient, and unconscious. The other is the "consequent nature" of God, the process of God's becoming by his collaboration with the temporal world, participating in the "creative advance of the world."[6] For the theologian Paul Tillich the ultimate God, which is being itself, is not unchanging or static, but has movement and becoming and lives creatively.

---

4. Bollas, *Forces*, 21.
5. Winnicott, "Communicating," 187.
6. Whitehead, *Process*, 406–14.

BEING AND THE SELF

Our psychological make up lends itself to preserve something indestructible in us. According to Winnicott a complete destruction of creative living is not possible. Hidden in the inner self is a secret life that is meaningful. This hidden part remains safe and original to that individual, even if compliance is extreme. That which proceeds from the true self is creative and original, and feels real. Reaction to environmental impingement feels unreal, futile.

The core is of great help in time of need. It may be likened to a Rock or a Redeemer that backs us up at times of great stress. This notion also appears in religions as the soul, or the Kabbalah's Yechidah, or the Hindu notion of Atman.

But that hidden core, according to Eigen, can turn destructive: "If one isolates a nuclear sense that others exist for oneself (if there are 'others'), to support one's life . . . one touches a thread that characterizes all pathology." The incommunicado core itself begins to change, "but not without memory of radiant innocence. A surviving background or trace of sweet goodness/innocence informs some of the most malignant, twisted cores."[7] The psychoanalyst Michael Eigen's expression "radiant innocence" brings to mind the Kabbalah's hidden divine sparks that break out of their imprisonment, penetrating the darkness "until the darkness itself shines, and there is no longer a division between the two."[8] Eigen's expansion of the idea of the core is an example of how he, like Winnicott, is averse towards closure and is open to exploration.

As indicated above, the idea of the hiddeness of our deepest part is drawn from religious sources. We attempt to discover the essence of ourselves while at the same time discovering the secret of the universe and of God. According to Thomas Merton, the Christian monk, our true self is not easy to find. It means that we have to recover an awareness of our inner identity, our true self, implying our realization that much of the time our everyday self is false. The true self is "hidden in obscurity and 'nothingness,' at the center where we are in direct dependence on God."[9] In Winnicott and Merton there is a surrendering of "guards." To liberate the true self there seems to be a surrendering of the false self with the risks that come with it—the fear of inner and outer attacks on enunciating "I am."

---

7. Eigen, *Flames*, 24.
8. Buber, *Tales*, 2:59.
9. Merton, *Contemplative Prayer*, 70.

PSYCHE, SOUL, AND SPIRIT

The true self, having shed the protective shell of the false self, feels everything intensely, including feelings of grief, dread, and hate, as well as love, joy, and peace. One of the poet Rainer Maria Rilke's intense experiences is his feeling that the things of the earth desire to be delivered from transitoriness, that one of our tasks is to praise these things and transform them:

> And these Things,
> which live by perishing, know you are praising them; transient,
> they look to us for deliverance: us the most transient of all.
> They want us to change them, utterly, in our invisible heart,
> within—oh endlessly—within us! Whoever we may be at last.[10]

Our being here, Rilke says, our presence in the world, is to bring alive the things of the earth, and to bring these things to life within us:

> Perhaps we are *here* in order to say: house,
> bridge, fountain, gate, pitcher, fruit-tree, window—
> at most: column, tower.... But to *say* them, you must understand,
> oh to say them *more* intensely than the Things themselves
> ever dreamed of existing.[11]

In discussing the true self Winnicott sees the need to enliven something in us that is dormant. Spontaneity in action, being felt in the body, is how this comes about. Rabbi Schneerson talks about a similar dormant state of our deepest part when he discusses the Yechidah. The Yechidah—which means "sole," the only one—is our essence, a personal divine spark in us that is imprisoned by inordinate desires and needs to be released. One's evolving soul abandons desire for the world and merges with the divine. The *Tanya*, the great work of the founder of Chabad-Lubavitch Hasidism, says that the essential core of the life force, which completely transcends the limitation of form, is a boundless essential energy.

As described by Winnicott, the false, compliant self is a necessary defense organization that originates in the infant's need to guard the spontaneity and creativity that belongs to its true self. However, living creatively, which is the only way to live satisfactorily, requires freedom from the false self. One needs to allow time and space for being, which means allowing a continuous flow that ends when there is a point of satisfaction in the creative process or in self-discovery.

---

10. Rilke, "Ninth Elegy," 201.
11. Ibid., 199.

Winnicott tightly links the true self and the false self, and alerts us that the purpose of formulating the true self is to try to understand the false self. It's in this comparison that the false self becomes clear as both as defense and as an aspect to the true self. "There is but little point in formulating a True Self idea except for the purpose of trying to understand the False Self, because it does no more than collect together the details of the experience of aliveness."[12]

The false self is bereft of a spontaneous gesture and lacks the stance of "I am that I am." The false self is crowded with people in one's head, people whom we are placating, distracting ourselves by being preoccupied with them. Winnicott expands the notion of the true self in healthy living to include a compliant aspect, where the infant is able to compromise so as not to be exposed. Surprisingly, according to Winnicott, this is an achievement. Compromise here is a sign of a true self strong enough to remain as oneself while compromising.

To live from the true self and elaborate on it we must be able to face the fact that we are alone. We are alone from the very beginning of life, in an essential aloneness, as Winnicott points out, that requires optimal conditions of which the infant is unaware—the support of the mother. This aloneness with an unknown background support persists in adult life especially when we are originating. According to Eigen there is a boundless aspect to that support—the unknown support of the experience of being, the unknown support of God. Without any overt reference to God as a supportive being, Winnicott uses terms through which one tastes religion/spirituality, terms such the *primary state of being, sacredness, support,* and *merging,* among others.

For Merton, the universe, including us, is at the mercy of God. All is dependent on God, and as such the self and being can only be discussed, not in psychological or metaphysical terms as did Winnicott and Whitehead, respectively, but rather in religious existential terms. Merton follows a calling and chooses solitude in his monastery, daring to plunge in the abyss of being, and when experiencing the power of the divine he feels great dread and awe. He talks of the dread we feel of the encounter of God, which may not be the way we envisioned it; the dread of losing oneself in God; and the dread of death—all of which exist in our deepest selves. His experience is subjective, yet several saints throughout the ages have gone through similar

12. Winnicott, "True and False Self," 148.

experiences. According to their testimony, when naked and stripped of worldliness the self, standing face to face with God, goes through a process of purging and renewal. Merton discusses surrendering to God, tolerating the dread that comes with it and the joy that issues from surviving it. What for Winnicott is the true self from which creativity emerges, for Merton is the self living only in God's love. Merton's renewed self comes about by the shedding of the old self, with its illusion of being separated from God, and the realization of our nothingness without him.[13] The terror that Rilke experiences also relates to a meeting with God:

> God speaks to each of us as he makes us, then walks with us silently out of the night.
>
> These are the words we dimly hear:
>
> You, sent out beyond your recall, go to the limits of your longing.
> Embody me.
> Flare up like a flame
> and make big shadows I can move in.
> Let everything happen to you: beauty and terror.
> Just keep going. No feeling is final.
> Don't let yourself lose me.
> Nearby is the country they call life.
> You will know it by its seriousness.
> Give me your hand.[14]

On meeting God, Abram undergoes a renewal. He falls into a deep sleep, and even though God attempts to reassure him of divine protection, terror seizes him. Abram's name is changed to Abraham, adding the Hebrew "h," which stands for God's unpronounceable name, and he is destined to become the father of many nations. Abraham, when undergoing this personal terrifying experience, comes across as an individual against the backdrop of a future tribal society. Winnicott says that the struggle to reach the concept of the human individual "is reflected, perhaps, in the early Hebrew name for God. . . . Does not this name (I AM) given to God reflect the danger that the individual feels he or she is in on reaching the state of individual being? . . . If I am, then I have gathered together this and that and have claimed it as me, and I have repudiated everything else; in

---

13. Merton, *Contemplative Prayer*, 122, 128.
14. Rilke, "Go to the Limits," 177, 201.

repudiating the not-me I have, so to speak, insulted the world, and I must expect to be attacked."[15]

Eigen notes that the biblical God "declares His name (or one of them) is 'I am' or 'I am I' or 'I will be what I will be' or 'I will be there.'"[16] The two first two names reflect being, the unchanging/conceptual nature of God that persists in the background and in some sense holds the universe together. The second two names reflect the becoming, the creative power of God that collaborates with our creative advance.

Tillich calls a sense of being an affirmation of the self, and he praises it by using the words "the courage to be" (the title of his book) to convey a sense of venture and perseverance in being oneself as an individual, including as a part of a group. This is to be in spite of an immense anxiety felt from the threat of nonbeing, which includes anxiety over guilt and judgment, meaninglessness and emptiness, fate and death. The courage of self-affirmation and the courage to die come from faith in "the God above the God of theism."[17] This is the God who is the power of being, Eigen's "unknown support." Tillich ends his book by saying, "*The courage to be is rooted in the God who appears when God has disappeared in the anxiety of doubt.*"[18] Akin to that is what the philosopher S. Alexander says: God is in the world and Deity is outside the world. Deity seems to be Tillich's God above God, the God who gives us courage to be. An example that Tillich uses is Socrates, who conquers the fear of death being certain that there is an aspect of his self that cannot be destroyed. Both religion and psychology, it seems, are attempting to dig deep inside to make contact with this inner indestructible essence of ourselves, which according to Winnicott is the foundation of meaningful creative living.

The reality of death faced boldly by Socrates reverberates in poems of Rilke, who does not flinch from presenting it straightforwardly:

> Of course, it is strange to inhabit the earth no longer,
> to give up customs one barely had time to learn,
> not to see roses and other promising Things
> in terms of a human future.[19]

---

15. Winnicott, *Home*, 57.
16. Eigen, *Contact*, 11.
17. Tillich, *Courage*, 186.
18. Ibid., 190.
19. Rilke, "First Elegy," 155.

PSYCHE, SOUL, AND SPIRIT

Rilke is fearless in his coming face to face with death, the side of life that is unilluminated, as Rilke calls it, and like Socrates, who envisions the indestructible aspect of ourselves, he presents us with a prospect of feeling "a trace of eternity."[20]

Merton's vision of the Christian life is to live in God, to lose oneself in God. The Sufi poet Rumi actualizes his longing to merge by uniting with the soul of his guru Shams:

> In thee the soul is dissolved, with thee it is mingled;
> Lo! I will cherish the soul, because it has the perfume of thee.
>
> Happy the moment when we are seated in the palace, thou and I,
> with two forms and with two figures, but with one soul, thou and I.[21]

When Rumi looked for Shams, whose body disappeared after being killed, he looked for him in a temple, on mountains, and in the Kaba, but couldn't find him, and then he came to the realization:

> I gazed into my heart;
> There I saw Him; He was nowhere else.[22]

According to the psychiatrist Arasteh, Rumi's search was for the site of the real self, culminated in finding it potentially within himself and actually within Shams. Though Rumi looked he didn't find it in religion or reason or other sources, as he says:

> I found love above idolatry and religion;
> I found love beyond doubt and reality.[23]

The love between Rumi and Shams facilitated an environment in which Rumi became one with Shams and in which the soul achieved a cosmic self. This unity is akin to Sri Ramana Maharshi's Self, with a capital "S," which is boundless, enlarging the small self to embrace others and all being. Maharshi is the Hindu saint who relates to the universal Self as the peak of the evolving self. This Self may take a lifetime or eons to achieve, and requires persistent spiritual effort and spiritual practice.

---

20. Ibid.
21. Arasteh, *Rumi*, 69–70.
22. Ibid., 69.
23. Ibid., 80.

BEING AND THE SELF

India has given the world great saints and heroes who have in common the strong belief that the desire to possess is unnatural and that human nature is inclined to renounce the separated self in favor of becoming one with others. The Maharshi devoted his life to helping others realize their true selves as one with the universal Self. He taught a process of inquiry—"Who am I?"—by which one dissolves the ego to achieve the Self. One expands beyond one's self-concern and self-absorption to embrace the Reality of Being, to be the Reality of Being. One is not different from this Reality.

In the teachings of the Maharshi, being is the state of realization of the ego-free self. The Maharshi's basic teaching is about discovering this ego-free self—the universal Self, the Self within—through a state of being. He was interested in the core of the person, the heart, the Self that is "waiting there to receive you." When a Western devotee questioned the Maharshi about one's duties, such as the duty to be a patriot, he answered, "Your duty is to be; and not to *be this or that*. 'I AM that I AM' sums up the whole truth. The method is summarized in BE STILL."[24]

According to the Maharshi, the most direct method of achieving the goal of realizing the Self is to ask oneself "Who am I?" and to hold on to this question. He tells us to ask this question when we feel an attachment that causes us to suffer. One fixes attention here, yet one will only achieve realization through a state of being in which thoughts and feelings will arise and free associations appear, but eventually are not allowed to remain. This practice, he thought, would result in a healing process and growth of the self. The small self will come to identify with the universal Self. To ask "Who am I?" means you are not fixed in, not closed off to what you think you are.

To ask the Maharshi's question "Who am I?" requires surrender, a "letting go" of patterns of thought and action, in the same way that one lets go of a desire to please and to comply and becomes involved in an activity of play that satisfies oneself alone. One surrenders the need to control one's destiny and the incorrect identification with the body or the ego. Serious inquiry into "Who am I?" would result in seeing that there is no such thing as "I" or "me." This vivid realization, as a direct and immediate experience of the supreme Truth, comes quite naturally, with nothing uncommon about it, to everyone who, remaining just as one is, enquires introspectively without allowing the mind even for a moment to become externalized or to waste time in mere talk.

---

24. Ramamasramam, *Maharshi*, 402.

PSYCHE, SOUL, AND SPIRIT

The Maharshi taught that one can achieve realization of the Self, accompanied by a perfect peace of withdrawal, even while active in the world, fulfilling work and familial requirements. He stressed the idea that the thought "It is I who is working" is what prevents the natural flow of being. The thought "I am doing this" immediately imposes certain standards of action and behavior and increases attachments to the results of that action or behavior. The ego resents certain results and retaliates against those who are in the way of attaining the desired results. The thought "I am this" is a reaction to the fear that if I am not somebody who can do this thing, then I am nothing. The focus of the Maharshi's teaching is on renouncing desires, passions, and attachments—giving up the small self. Even God, in the Maharshi's view, is detached:

> God has no purpose. He is not bound by any action. The world's activities cannot affect Him. Take the analogy of the sun. The sun rises without desire, purpose or effort, but as soon as it rises numerous activities take place on earth: the lens placed in its rays produces fire in its focus, the lotus bud opens, water evaporates, and every living creature enters upon activity, maintains it, and finally drops it. But the sun is not affected by any such activity, as it merely acts according to its nature, by fixed laws, without any purpose, and is only a witness. So it is with God.[25]

The "I" thought is the ego, whereas the real "I" is "I am that I am," a continuity of being. If I am "me" I see the world as external and am at risk of being affected by what happens. If I am the Self I am identical with the world and others; what happens does not happen to "me." Only through being—when we are not stirred up by thoughts—can we achieve this state. People who came to the Maharshi for relief of suffering were taught to cease identifying with their suffering self, which is not their Self. For example, the griever needs to ask, "Who is doing the grieving?" Similarly, when other thoughts and feelings interfere a person should not pursue them but should inquire, "To whom did they arise? All suffering, he said, is connected with the false thought that "I am this body" or "I am this ego."

Making use of the Maharshi's teachings requires trust in the unconscious and belief in the support that life itself provides. There is a need to abandon the inclination to consciously insert purpose into one's actions—an ingrained habit in Westerners. It is a particularly difficult transformation: to be the Self without thought; to immerse in the experience of the

---

25. Osborne, *Maharshi*, 87–88.

heart; to experience rather than to know; to be silent and still; to renounce wanting (not to want is frightening), thinking, achieving; to let being be a fresh anchorage, on which all doing would depend. One would have an existence that is not contingent on what one does. The asking of the question "Who Am I?" in order to receive the Self transitions one from a routine state to a dynamic one. This suggests a paradoxical dynamic stillness, and in this state the Maharshi's stance is redolent of psychological, religious, and philosophical notions presented here: seeking the true self, seeking God, becoming, and process. This state emanates unceasing power; it is a state that includes spontaneity, which is possible, according to Winnicott, in a safe environment (as it was originally) that fosters the growth of one's inherited potential. For Merton it is the grace of God that will rescue our spontaneity from a constrained life of routine into which we may fall unintentionally—a grace for which we must wait patiently.[26]

Being is as natural as a child at play. In early childhood play, according to Winnicott, there is a state of being in which the child arranges and rearranges objects, a process in which the child expresses and discovers his or her self. In this highly concentrated state, which is not easily interrupted, the child communicates with himself or herself. In a broader sense this characterization of play continues into adulthood, where the objects can be words, ideas, images, and colors, as well as physical materials, which are recombined into new patterns, entailing an inward-directed concentration and attention, spontaneous and free of self-consciousness. The Maharshi said that a child and a sage are alike, for both are interested in incidents only as long as they last, and are not affected by them mentally. The child and the adult in this state are allowing the unconscious impulses of the true self to be expressed and to remain.

The deep quest for the Self—God in each one of us, or each one a part of God—involves a freedom that one finds in play. Results are not externally imposed; the guru involved in instructing one on this path practices a restraint; he does not interfere, nor does he intervene with any expectations of his own, thus facilitating an environment that permits one's quest to take place at one's own pace. The Maharshi (who was addressed as Bhagavan, Blessed One) was free of self-interest and did not coerce or interrupt his devotee's life process:

---

26. Merton, *Contemplative Prayer*, 88.

PSYCHE, SOUL, AND SPIRIT

>Devotee. How to realize the Self?
>
>Bhagavan. Whose Self? Find out.
>
>D. Who am I?
>
>B. Find it yourself.
>
>D. I do not know.
>
>B. Think. Who is it that says "I do not know"? What is not known? In that statement, who is the "I"?
>
>D. Somebody in me.
>
>B. Who is that somebody? In whom?
>
>D. May be some power.
>
>B. Find it.[27]

The Maharshi's restraint encourages authenticity, in which the entire mind turns inward not to thought but to the source of thought.

The Maharshi was a trusted person, a nurturing figure who understood instinctively that, like a good-enough mother, one must concern oneself, as Winnicott said, with very subtle details of handling. The Maharshi exemplified being. He encouraged faith in him as a benign psychic presence for his devotees, one that *is*, allowing them to *be* also. Silence and stillness, with an added element of grace, was the Maharshi's primary form of instruction; he taught that the guru's silence gives room to the seeker's mind to purify itself. For those who can tolerate it, silence is a powerful way to transmit compassion and care, thus facilitating the experience of being. It bypasses the mind's constructions and interferences, which are manifestations of the "I" thought.

When the Maharshi's devotees asked questions, he stressed the value of his psychic presence, and was not intimidated or induced by their pressure to enter into their intellectual mode:

>Devotee. Can Sri Bhagavan help us to realize the Truth?
>
>Bhagavan. Help is always there.
>
>D. Then, there is no need to ask questions. I do not feel the ever-present help.

---

27. Ramanasramam, *Maharshi*, 71–72.

BEING AND THE SELF

B. Surrender and you will find it.

D. I am always at your feet. Will Bhagavan give us some upadesa (instruction) to follow? Otherwise, how can I get the help living 600 miles away?

B. The Sad Guru (true teacher) is within.

D. The Sad Guru is necessary to guide me to understand it.

B. That Sad Guru is within.

D. I want a visible Guru.

B. That visible Guru says that He is within.[28]

To the question of how can one know whether a particular person is competent to be a guru, the Maharshi answered, "By the peace of mind you feel in his presence and by the respect you feel for him."[29]

Winnicott served as a benign psychic presence for his patients. He was not "this or that," clever or superior to them; his job was to be himself. He was there "to afford opportunity for formless experience, and for creative impulses, motor and sensory, which are the stuff of playing."[30] He described two sessions, amounting to five hours, in which a patient was gradually able to move away from despair over feeling that she didn't matter to anyone (including herself) and feeling "not quite able to be." Throughout, Winnicott was mostly silent, submitting to the patient's process, without impinging on it by making his own interpretations. At one point the patient associated "something good" with the wish to be, while expressing a fear of being. She was then able to move to making her own interpretations, realizing that the wish to be good, to please the analyst, implied a wish not to get well, to continue to be a compliant false self, a "good girl." Toward the end of the second session the patient asked Winnicott a question, to which he responded, "You had the idea to ask that question." After this, "She said, slowly, with deep feeling, 'Yes, I see, one could postulate the existence of a ME from the question, as from the searching.'"[31]

Eigen remembers Winnicott being as himself:

---

28. Ibid., 489.
29. Ibid., 288.
30. Winnicott, *Playing*, 64.
31. Ibid.

> I met Winnicott near the end of his life, his creativity in full bloom, I was left with a profound sense that if he could be him, I could be me. He was so himself, quirky, awkward, unapologetic about his intensity, that it freed me to be more myself. A deep kind of permission that if a sensibility like his could exist, then a sensibility like mine could, too. This may sound presumptuous, but it springs from his need to share his own sensibility, his sense of reality, a spontaneous striving.[32]

Winnicott and the Maharshi made the point that what is sought—the true self or the universal Self—is already there inside the person. Winnicott spoke of the state of being emerging out of not being. He pointed out that we can return to not being, unintegration, at any age in order to begin again. This concept provides insight into the psychological process that is involved in the quest for identity, even of a spiritual nature. The concept helps us see what may be involved in using the Maharshi's practice of persistent questioning of who one is. The Maharshi's teachings shed light on Winnicott's view and practice, however different their world hypotheses; repeated examination of who one is is a practice that questions the validity of the false self, catching it at work and arresting it, thus allowing the true self to live.

There seems to be a consensus among the sources we have cited that inside each one of us is an unexpressed, hidden and buried, essence that is crying out to be and become a self that is alive. The consensus holds true also for the concepts of being and becoming—for the dynamism in both, for the courage it takes to be as oneself, for the courage to face death, for living creatively anew each day—a life that requires unending hard work.

---

32. Eigen, *Faith*, 15.

4

MILAREPA AND DEMONS: AIDS TO SPIRITUAL AND PSYCHOLOGICAL GROWTH[1]

> ABSTRACT: *Milarepa, the Tibetan Buddhist saint of the eleventh century, wrote songs that give expression to a methodology of battling internal resistance to spiritual growth. The songs provide a meticulous description of how a person beset by demons processes and analyzes his behavior, thus enabling him to assess them correctly and objectively. At the start Milarepa perceives his demons as invaders, thereby disavowing responsibility for them. But later he is able to recognize their presence in his mind, thus avowing responsibility for them and releasing them, and even converting them. Throughout the songs Milarepa is attacked by demons, and he calls on his gurus and other mental companions to help him battle them. The demons are obvious obstacles, but Milarepa uses them to strengthen himself in his spiritual progress. These processes have psychological equivalents relevant to Westerners.*

SPIRITUAL AND PSYCHOLOGICAL JOURNEYS almost always encounter opposition. In Tibetan Buddhism the opposition sometimes is represented by demons that act to distract monks and nuns in their meditation. A belief in demons is not an essential feature of Buddhist thought, however, Tibetan Buddhism accommodated itself to popular demonology and made creative use of it.

Milarepa, an eleventh-century Tibetan adept, and a remarkable, original, and colorful storyteller, describes his spiritual trials in the classic work *The Hundred Thousand Songs of Milarepa*. The tales of his journey exhibit a theory of demons and describe an untiring practice, a path of spiritual growth, from the point of view of the pilgrim. Milarepa, who in his past killed many people—innocent as well as harmful—to avenge wrongs done to his family, is redeeming his life by his struggle with demons. In his songs Milarepa depicts his experiences with demons—evil, malign beings whose

---

1. Originally published in the *Journal of Religion and Health* 40/3 (Fall 2001) 371–82.

destructive natures are due to bad karma, and who assault him as he makes progress in his spiritual practice.

The psychologist Mark Finn, in his illuminating paper "Transitional Space and Tibetan Buddhism: The Object Relations of Meditation," addresses the interpenetration of the spiritual and the psychodynamic, as revealed in Milarepa's song "The Tale of Red Rock Jewel Valley." We begin our discussion with the same song, the most complete expression of Milarepa processing his demons and arriving at the understanding that they are manifestations of his internal impediments. His struggle with demons, when examined from a psychological perspective, provides insights and casts light on the concept of internal objects, good and bad. Like Finn we discuss the process of conjuring up the lost good object—psychological support for personal growth—and avowing and releasing bad objects, as depicted in "The Tale of Red Rock." The theme of our paper is Milarepa's interaction with demons, which, though they are obstacles distracting and hindering him from making progress, are the very tools that make him aware of his need to work harder in his Buddhist meditation practice. The notion of psychic attacks, the equivalence of demons and their impact on us, is examined. We stress and elaborate on the concept of benign psychic and physical presences as companions, and also on the importance of having confidence in one's goodness as a base for avowing badness, as we trace Milarepa's further development indicated in other songs.

In the beginning of "The Tale of Red Rock," Milarepa is absorbed in practicing his meditation and suddenly feels pangs of hunger. He interrupts his meditation in order to look for food, collects some twigs, and is confronted by a sudden storm. He tries to hold on to his robe, and the wood is blown away. He tries to clutch the wood, and the robe is blown away. Frustrated, he becomes aware that he is not rid of ego clinging, even though he has been living in solitude for a long time, practicing the Dharma. (Dharma refers to the teachings of Buddha. Ego clinging refers to the erroneous idea that one is an independently arising being, and, as the Dalai Lama teaches, also refers to a tendency inherited from one's karma to reinforce the self by attachments to the results of worldly experiences.)

Having become aware of his ego clinging, Milarepa is critical of himself: "What is the use of practicing Dharma if one cannot subdue ego-clinging?"[2] To Milarepa there is a glaring incongruity in devoting time and effort to meditating on the non-existence of the substance of beings—the

---

2. Chang, *Milarepa*, 1.

ungraspable nature of all existence—yet grasping things. He instantaneously decides to let the wind do what it will: blow away his robe, blow away the wood.

When the storm is over, Milarepa sees a shred of his clothing swaying on a branch of a tree. The ephemeral quality of the cloth offers itself to Milarepa as a symbol of the trifling quality of the world, the meaninglessness and uselessness of worldly concerns. He realizes anew "the utter futility of this world and all its affairs,"[3] and responds by renouncing again his attachment to the things of the world. This reaffirmation is another step towards Nirvana, the Supreme Peace that is the goal of Buddhism.

Milarepa returns to his meditation but is soon distracted by thoughts of his guru, Marpa, and Marpa's wife. He has been living in a cave for a long time alone, yet accompanied by the continued internalized presence of Marpa, which has helped him in his solitude, supporting his practices of renunciation. Now he is tormented by the absence of Marpa's physical presence; the internalized presence is not enough—a state induced by the new level of his spiritual development. He pleads for Marpa's support, and to conjure him up sings "Thoughts of My Guru," in which he expresses intense suffering:

> Though in my deepest faith and veneration
> I have never been apart from you,
> I am now tortured by my need to see you.
> This fervent longing agonizes me,
> This great torment suffocates me.
> Pray, my gracious Guru, relieve me from this torment.[4]

Milarepa's painful longing to be with Marpa, physically or imaginatively, the tormenting loneliness that he experiences, is an example of what the psychoanalyst Melanie Klein refers to in her essay "The Sense of Loneliness." She observes that we mistakenly attribute our sense of loneliness to our relationship with the outside world: "It is generally supposed that loneliness can derive from the conviction that there is no person or group to which one belongs. This not belonging can be seen to have a much deeper meaning. However much integration proceeds, it cannot do away with the feeling that certain components of the self are not available because they are split off and cannot be regained."[5] According to Klein, these split-off

---

3. Ibid.
4. Ibid., 3.
5. Klein, "Loneliness," 302.

components include bad parts as well as good parts of the self and one's loneliness is a clue to the lack of integration of these parts. In Milarepa's case, he longs to integrate his good object—to reconnect with the original good mother through connecting with his outside supportive figure, his Guru and teacher Marpa.

Milarepa was initially sent into solitude by Marpa as a way of reaching deeper into himself, into attachments and longings, and to strengthen his commitment to the Buddhist goal of liberation. The practice of solitude creates an increased capacity to rely upon his own resources for his spiritual growth and eventually then to help others in their spiritual development. In his song to Marpa, Milarepa is praying for help as another means of gathering strength for the battle against destructiveness. Marpa responds to Milarepa's pleading. He appears to him "on a cluster of rainbow clouds,"[6] and is quick to judge his longing as rooted in an experience of doubt and destructiveness—non-Dharmic thoughts originating in the belief in the reality of the substance of things and the desire to attain them. In response to Milarepa's call for his support, Marpa admonishes him: "Why do you struggle so? Have you not an abiding faith in your Guru and Patron Buddha? Does the outer world attract you with disturbing thoughts? Do fear and longing sap your strength?"[7] Marpa reminds Milarepa that he is always with him, providing encouragement for his continued efforts in pursuing his goal: "No matter what the cause, you may be certain that we will never part. Thus, for the sake of the Dharma and the welfare of sentient beings continue your meditation."[8]

Milarepa is stirred by Marpa's words and the vision of his countenance. Having perceived the good object outside himself, he now experiences it inside himself:

> His [Marpa's] compassionate blessings enter me;
> all destructive thoughts are banished.[9]

Milarepa returns to his path and reminds himself of the value of his goal; as an act of gratitude to his Guru, he offers him his unconquerable steadfastness:

> Indomitable perseverance

6. Chang, *Milarepa*, 3.
7. Ibid.
8. Ibid., 3–4.
9. Ibid., 4.

MILAREPA AND DEMONS

Is the highest offering to my Guru.[10]

Milarepa consolidates his resolve by making further declarations: enduring the hardship of meditation is "the best way to please Him [the Guru]," and abiding alone in the cave "is the noblest service to the Dakinis [goddesses]!" He prays to Marpa to help him stay in the hermitage: "Pray, pity me and grant me your protection!"[11] The good object is reinstated simultaneously with an experience of gratitude and an expression of that gratitude and of homage to a teacher and spiritual director.

Milarepa acknowledges that he owes his strength to the support that Marpa has given him during this time:

> Father Guru, who conquered the Four Demons,
> I bow to you, Marpa the Translator....
> Though demons, ghosts, and devils multiply,
> I am not afraid.[12]

["The Four Demons" that had been conquered by Marpa are the four major hindrances to spiritual progress—illness, interruption, death, and desires and passions.]

The value of calling on good companions appears in other songs. Milarepa makes contact with other benign psychic presences, which help him build and strengthen confidence in his goodness. In "The Song of Good Companions" he lists "one-and-twenty good companions," beginning with his Gurus, whom he likens to a string of jewels. He has three companions for prayer—the Gurus, Patron Buddhas and Dakinis—and among others, companions for refuge, for learning, for practice, for meditation, and for escorts through whom to conquer hindrances. In "The Holy Gambopa—Milarepa's Foremost Disciple," Milarepa teaches how to call forth the companionship of one's Guru:

> Visualize Him upon your head
> And for His blessing pray.
> Visualize Him sitting
> In the center of your heart,
> And forget Him never.[13]

---

10. Ibid.
11. Ibid., 6–7.
12. Ibid.
13. Ibid., 492.

Milarepa refers to his spiritual family as additional mental supports (or good objects): His father is the "All-Perfect-One," his aunt, the "Lamp-of-Illumination." Calling forth supports is an example for us: when we are in need we can *call up* our own companions, teachers, friends, mentors.

We now return to "The Tale of Red Rock." Milarepa, having fortified his determination by praying to Marpa, returns to his cave to "meditate and meditate again." He is exalted. This happy experience, however, does not last. He is "startled to find five Indian demons with eyes as large as saucers."[14] It is significant that the demons appear to him after he has achieved some measure of success in his meditation. Milarepa assumes that the demons are benign: "one was sitting on his bed and preaching, two were listening to the sermon, another was preparing and offering food, and the last was studying Milarepa's books."[15] Thinking that these demons must be "magical apparitions of the local deities," who dislike him for neglecting to give them "any offering or compliment," he placates them with a song describing the beauty and serenity of their province, suggesting that they drink "the nectar of kindness and compassion"[16] and leave.

The philosopher Herbert Fingarette, in his discussion of self-deception, provides insight into Milarepa's psychological state. Milarepa either finds the appearance of demons in his cave so painful to accept that he purposely induces the belief that it is not so; or in an innocent type of self-deception, he believes the "apparitions of local deities" to be what they appear. As we noted Milarepa suggests that the demons leave. The demons not only do not leave but they manifest their true nature: "Two of them advanced, one grimacing and biting his lower lip, and the other grinding his teeth horribly. A third, coming up behind, gave a violent, malicious laugh and shouted loudly, as they all tried to frighten Milarepa with fearful grimaces and gestures."[17] Milarepa meditates and recites a powerful incantation to remove these malevolent demons, but they do not leave. He preaches the Dharma to them with great compassion, but to no avail.

Milarepa sees the demons as invaders: he disavows his responsibility for them. This disavowal is analogous to the psychoanalytic disavowal of one's badness. Though he has progressed far in his spiritual development, Milarepa is not ready to acknowledge that the demons are his; to do so would

14. Ibid., 4.
15. Ibid.
16. Ibid., 5.
17. Ibid.

have required relinquishing the affirmation of his personal integrity as a good object. Fingarette describes the phenomenon of disavowal: "Isolation, non-responsibility, and the incapacity to spell-out, with the consequences in turn attendant upon these, constitute three chief dimensions of disavowal, three profoundly significant defects of personal integrity."[18] (Note the paradox inherent in using terms such as *self-deception* and *personal integrity* in the context of the Buddhist claim of the unreality of the self.)

After attempting to get rid of the demons outwardly, Milarepa is struck anew by the realization that all struggles take place in one's mind: "I have already fully realized that all beings and all phenomena are of one's own mind. The mind itself is a transparency of Voidness. [Psychologically, *Voidness* means a complete liberation from all bondage to one's projections and to one's internal objects.] What, therefore, is the use of all this, and how foolish I am to try to dispel these manifestations physically!"[19] In a shift similar to the way he experienced the good object, Milarepa turns his focus of attention from what appears to be the enemy to the actual enemy, the one within. This change of focus occurs after he has exhausted all his means of removing the external obstacles to his practice of meditation and after he has called upon Marpa and internalized him.

Reinstating the good object and the security it restores—confidence in his goodness and in his skills—allows Milarepa to admit that his demons are his own. Klein points out that the feeling of goodness is accompanied by the feeling that destructive impulses will not overwhelm love. One then can tolerate deficiencies in oneself. Winnicott discusses a case in which a patient was able to acknowledge negative feelings only after having expressed a constructive aim.

When Milarepa realizes that the demons exist in his mind, he is undaunted. He sings "The Song of Realization," emphasizing his fearlessness and proclaiming his devotion to Buddhist teachings, remaining true to his nature, which like the eagle "never falls down from the sky."[20] After all, he has dedicated his life to eradicating the demons within! Nevertheless, Milarepa playfully invites them to battle with him, and he rushes straight at them as if he still thinks they exist outside of him. Now it is the demons who are frightened. They shrink back, rolling their eyes in despair, trembling violently. "Swirling together like a whirlpool, they all merged into

18. Fingarette, *Self-Deception*, 74.
19. Chang, *Milarepa*, 5.
20. Ibid., 7.

one and vanished."[21] Milarepa has completed the hard work of conquering the demons in his mind, and he reestablishes his identity as someone who from birth has been suffused with Buddhist teachings. Then comes an afterthought, a moment of quietude in which Milarepa's conscience rewards him. He succeeds in identifying his distraction by name: "This was the demon king Vinayaka, the Obstacle Maker, who came searching for evil opportunities," he thought, "the storm too is undoubtedly his creation." With deference and gratitude to Marpa, he recognizes Marpa's hand in preventing harm. He thereafter gains "immeasurable spiritual progress."[22]

It may be argued that in the first part of his life Milarepa is paranoid-schizoid: having been fearful of internal persecutors and subsequently projecting his badness onto an outside object, he is dominated and damaged by this object. With the help of Marpa and his wife, figures who helped Milarepa reconnect with his original good object, he has transformed his paranoid-schizoid personality to a schizoid one—still separated from his bad parts, indicated by the fact that he experiences them as objects of conquest. Rushing at the demons, mocking and belittling them, and conquering them could be said to indicate a manic solution, evidence of disavowing one's badness—a resolution short of the integration that belongs to the depressive position, in which there is a progression from guilt and concern to reparation. From the Buddhist perspective, however, the practice includes consciously engaging in a physical as well as a mental activity. Milarepa often crosses the boundaries between inside and outside of himself, creating a constant tension and interaction between the two. His goal is to achieve the realization that his "hindrances are but a shadow-show" and to remove them as obstacles. Rushing at the demons until they vanish is a portrayal of that practice, albeit a primitive one. It also could be seen as a playful ending to the tale, a literary device.

The Buddhist perspective and most of Western psychology emphasize focusing on internal opposition to growth. The psychoanalyst Edoardo Weiss talks about attacks that are in one's mind; he discusses persecuting psychic presences, powerful mental attitudes of people who are close to us that control and override our way of feeling and thinking in a situation. According to the psychoanalyst Dr. Preston G. McLean, psychic attacks also may originate in a group of people (more rarely one person) not close to oneself who want to destroy one's progress out of spoiling envy or hate.

21. Ibid.
22. Ibid.

MILAREPA AND DEMONS

Sometimes we experience these attacks upon entering "new territory," an act perceived as a threat by its present occupants. The attacks are experienced as sudden feelings of worthlessness, helplessness, or even fear of impending annihilation. They may be so severe that, unless we identify these groups or persons, we may be blocked from moving forward. Such attacks afflict Milarepa in the form of demons who say, for example:

> We have come to take your life, your soul, and spirit;
> To stop your breath and take consciousness from
> your body.[23]

The psychoanalyst D. W. Winnicott characterizes attackers as those who see psychological health as unattainable for themselves, who want to destroy those who attain this health: "The amount of resentment that accumulates in this area is terrific and corresponds to the well person's sense of guilt about being well." As a result the "haves" feverishly organize themselves into helping the "have-nots."[24]

As Milarepa progresses he becomes more skillful in realizing that demons and manifestations in the cosmos are created by himself:

> Fictions conjured up by mind,
> Manifest yet non-existent.[25]

In the song "The Goddess Tserinma's Attack" Milarepa is again visited by demons: "The eighteen Great Demons, leading all the ghosts and spirits in the whole Universe, came to attack him in order to hinder his devotion." Milarepa does not succumb to his first impression of them, enabling him to assess them correctly and objectively. He immediately realizes their nature and their purpose:

> The ghosts and Devas in the Realms of form
> Are all assembled here; none is left out.
> Most eminent among them are the five female demons
> Who into dread and hideous shapes have turned.
> They have come to hinder my devotion,
> And seek occasion [to distract me].
> I see a demoness grin like a skeleton,
> And lift up Mount Sumeru;
> I see a red one put out her tongue which drips with

---

23. Ibid., 300.
24. Winnicott, "Freedom," 234–35.
25. Chang, *Milarepa*, 304.

blood
And swallow the ocean waters.[26]

Demons attempt to lure Milarepa, the spiritual pilgrim, to the manifest world, knowing that generally they can exploit human attachment to it. They believe they can undermine his reliance on benign mental companions. They attempt to sow seeds of confusion in his mind about the value of his commitment. Milarepa hears them laughing: "Ha, Ha! The foundation of his wisdom is collapsing!"[27] Milarepa is not shaken by the demons' appearance; he knows what to do—summon the "guards of Dharma" to protect and help him. He prays to supporting figures such as the Patron Buddha, his gurus, and the Wrathful Deities—his mental army—to destroy the "nets and snares" of the demons. The demons take this to mean that Milarepa has lost his peace of mind, and they test his achievement in yoga by singing the "Proclamation of the Hindrances," in which they insult and threaten him. Milarepa's intense determination and devotion, the extreme seriousness with which he meditates, is matched by an intense and ferocious attack. The demons deride his place of meditation as dark and perilous, a lonely path, difficult and hazardous, and attempt to dissuade him from staying there by pointing out that he will be proceeding without companions.

Milarepa once again refers to the demons as conjurations of his own mind. The fact that he has conjured them up indicates that they are his own inner obstructions. Though they are manifestations, they need to be confronted as if they really exist. He recalls that, unlike his own mind, the nature of Mind is the Illuminating Essence and that these demons are not part of this indestructible nature. Milarepa consolidates his realization that demons are delusory and therefore non-threatening—a sample of the delusory nature of existence in general:

> All life is transient and changeable . . . the perception of the afflicter and the afflicted is as delusory as clouds, mist, and flickering mirages seen through impaired eyes. These delusory visions are like "veils" created by wavering thoughts, which themselves have been produced by habitual thinking derived from Original Blindness since beginningless time in Samsara [the wheel of life and death].[28]

---

26. Ibid., 297.
27. Ibid., 298.
28. Ibid., 301.

MILAREPA AND DEMONS

"Habitual thinking" brings to mind the rigidity of psychological defenses against taking the risk of change. Our need for safety can disrupt our efforts to advance creatively. For example, something may make perfect sense for us to do, and suddenly we are plagued by doubt. This psychic attack can be an alarm signal that reminds us of our initial plan and prompts us to implement what we had in mind.

When the demons become aware of Milarepa's resolve, they regret their attempts to distract him and sing to him about his merits. Milarepa has converted them. The demons warn him against further possible demonic attractions and distractions. Milarepa points out that demonic obstacles are not entirely evil, and stresses that yogis use them as opportunities for growth. He now makes use of demons as supports to build his strength, helping him reaffirm the value of his path and orienting him to the need to counter his own destructive thoughts. He likens demonic obstacles to the cracks of a horsewhip—stimulants for indolent beginners. For enlightened practitioners, demons are guardians of Buddha's teachings:

> The malignant
> Male and female demons
> Who create myriad troubles and obstructions,
> Seem real before one has Enlightenment;
> But when one realizes their nature truly,
> They become Protectors of the Dharma,
> And by their help and [freely given] assistance
> One attains to numerous accomplishments.[29]

Milarepa has transformed malignant demons into aids for spiritual growth.

Another example of the transformation of demons appears in "The Conversion of the Goddess Tserinma." Milarepa is singing to Tserinma and her companions. He reminds them that they had caused the demon army to harm him. He points out that he had not been frightened:

> By merely seeing you poor sinful beings,
> An unbearable compassion, quite beyond control,
> Rose of itself within me.[30]

The demons, by evoking compassion, have helped him achieve one of the highest Buddhist virtues. Milarepa's benign attitude towards his own demons points to wisdom and a sense of peace.

29. Ibid., 309.
30. Ibid., 320.

PSYCHE, SOUL, AND SPIRIT

Tibetan Buddhism developed a whole spectrum of demons that become real and alive as they reflect varieties of badness and the opposite types of goodness. When destroying or neutralizing evil and replacing it with good, Milarepa adapts his methods to the nature of the evil, as he describes in the "The Conversion of a Dying Bonist." For the absence of self-awareness he offers self-renunciation; to cleanse clinging to self and egotism he makes altruistic offerings. He performs a dance called "The Voidness of Mental Functions" to nullify habitual thinking. He advocates responsibility for destructive feelings by acknowledging "fire-like angry demons" and "poisoning" them with "The Wisdom of Void."[31] Milarepa instructs his listeners to go beyond acknowledging destructive feelings: to eliminate them by generating virtues such as wisdom and compassion. He himself is prepared to do the ultimate—offer his body as ransom for humankind—as a way to clear the debts and bad karma he accumulated in his early life.

The capacity to recognize our demons as our own, appearances notwithstanding, is crucial to the transformation of our badness. Eigen, in the epilogue to "Toxic Nourishment," says, "Only after I was married did it dawn on me with crystalline authority that my relationships [with many girlfriends] had been tortured because *I* was tortured. Yes, *I* was the red thread that ran through my life."[32] Ignoring our interior obstacles allows them to become more habitual and cause more damage. Milarepa's determination and his commitment to identifying and nullifying the hindrances to his spiritual progress give us an example and permission to do likewise. The movements and shifts in Milarepa's mind are testimony to his struggle with the distracting force of demons: he shifts from being absorbed to being distracted, to feeling attacked and lonely, to feeling supported while attacked, and finally to combating the attack and reinstating fearlessness, regaining momentum in spiritual progress. A prerequisite to that determination is a staunch belief in the good object in him, illusory as it may be.

Milarepa's experience helps us focus on our interior life. Meditation, prayer, calling on mental companions, and processing the workings of our psyche are the resources we have to tap into our good objects, to help us be aware of when we are denying and projecting our bad objects, and to identify our bad objects by name. Tolerance towards our bad impulses, which weakens our projections, leads us to tolerate other people's defects. According to

---

31. Ibid., 247–48.
32. Eigen, *Toxic*, 214–15.

MILAREPA AND DEMONS

Eigen, we can even make creative use of our "fatal flaws." Character defects that we are stuck with can result in character strengthening.

The Buddhist belief in demons facilitates the creation of elaborate powerful descriptions of sins that give them shape and form, life, flavor, color and actuality, pictorial or emotional expression. These descriptions reach the unconscious; they trigger an immediate emotional response and facilitate awareness of the existence of hidden destructive energy. Milarepa in one of his songs sings about "feeding my little child, 'Awareness.'" The practice of developing awareness—identifying and naming our bad objects, and even giving them pictorial form—can be a methodology for psychological growth. For example, paranoid feelings can be embodied as our own demoness putting out her tongue that drips with blood. In "The Conversion of a Dying Bonist," demons are let loose on a dying man's family, sending forth forceful afflictions such as "burning anger," "stirring lust," "blind ignorance," "stinging jealousy," "self-praise and self-inflation," and "evil deeds and habitual-thinking,"[33] all of whose evil power is dreadful, pernicious, and fierce. Demons enable us to recognize and identify sins by sight, which leaves no doubt as to their existence and induces an urgency to neutralize or destroy them, or transform them.

The obstacles that Milarepa has transmuted into aids for spiritual growth are vehicles for "nourishment of wisdom." In "The Journey to Lashi" he deems his demons glorious: "To me, the afflictions and obstructions caused by demons are the glories of a yogi's mind. The greater such affliction, the more I gain in the Path of Bodhi."[34] [The Path of Bodhi is the path that leads to Buddhahood.]

Demons attack Milarepa because of his indefatigable progress in his practice. Milarepa praises the very phenomenon of demons:

> Again, the foolish concept "demons" itself
> Is groundless, void and yet illuminating!
> Oh, this indeed is marvelous and wonderful![35]

From a religious perspective as well as a psychological one, a demonic or a psychic attack could be a validation of the value of one's goal and the progress one is making towards its achievement. The attack indicates that it is important to take this direction, to continue what we are doing, and

---

33. Chang, *Milarepa*, 246.
34. Ibid., 14.
35. Ibid., 310.

not, as we are inclined to assume, to cease doing it. We need optimal persecution—not too much and not too little—to energize us, to awaken us to renew our commitment, and to excel.

5

MILAREPA ON DETACHMENT AND WORLDLINESS

The Tibetan Buddhist yogi Milarepa knew the world and human passions by acquaintance. As a youth he had great love for and attachment to his mother, who had suffered grievous wrongs from her relatives and, in her rage and desire for revenge, persuaded Milarepa to use his powers to destroy them. Remorse for these acts was the turning point in Milarepa's life. Determined to make reparation, he found a guru to help him on a spiritual journey so that he could achieve enlightenment and be of service to others.

A key Buddhist teaching is detachment from the world, using the motivation that any engagement with the world results in suffering. Ego-clinging, a self-regarding attitude, is at the base of any attachment to people and objects in the world. To rid himself of ego-clinging Milarepa leaves the world and its worldliness and lives in nature. There he has a solitary, contact-free environment in which to process and finally extinguish his desires and meditate upon the "void-illuminating Mind," the primordial nature of mind, from which "both pure and impure thoughts are cleared, as in a silver mirror."[1] Even in the natural environment he struggles to renounce his desire for a bit of comfort, such as the garment he wears and the wood he burns for warmth in the winter, recognizing each bit of desire as ego-clinging. Milarepa's renunciation of the world is radical, as is his detachment from his ego.

This renunciation of the world, the struggles and rewards of Milarepa's spiritual journey, and his teachings are described in his "Hundred Thousand Songs." We, his enthusiastic readers, read his songs for sheer joy, for their bold descriptions of nature and for his perspicuity in regard to people and the world. In them we recognize our significant and petty attachments, the

1. Chang, *Milarepa*, 437.

inevitability of the suffering involved in our attachments, the senselessness of our fears and terrors. We see clearly how keeping the company of people leads to strife and how easily we become enslaved to our desires for possessions. Above all we read Milarepa in order to be touched by his strange and wondrous saintly life, and to study and apply his spirituality to our lives on the level that we can or want. The teachings that pervade his songs are useful reminders for those of us who are concerned with developing our spirituality. Though it is unlikely that any of us will apply his extreme view that the world is an illusion, which requires complete abandonment of the world, we may use his teachings that are on the level of our everyday lives.

While the world may see Milarepa as "doing nothing," Milarepa is very busy "taming the wild goats" of his desires, "subduing the demon Ego," and feeding his "little child, Awareness"; he has no time to make money in the world because he is "gathering the Dharma wealth" or "herding the steeds of Self-awareness."[2] He is involved in practices that include watching his mind, absorbing himself in self-awareness, eliminating search and aspiration; in more aggressive practices such as subduing habitual thinking, striving for altruistic deeds, and telling the truth; and in evolved practices such as seeing that manifestations in existence are conducive rather than obstructive to spiritual growth.

In his songs Milarepa resolves to meet any challenge that opposes his spiritual evolution, whether it is the villagers whose worldliness he considers worse than death, his own clinging to anything that even slightly smacks of the world, or the logicians and theologians who come to debate with him. In one of his most telling songs we learn that worldliness not only thrives in the marketplace but in more subtle ways in the scholarly world, which, like the materialistic world, is hostile to and jealous of the spiritual life. Milarepa, having fully mastered the Mind-realms of himself and others, "remained happily in the Belly Cave of Nya Non to help sentient beings."[3] While his fame spread, scholars-monks of the Nya Non monastery declared him a heretic. They consider ousting him, and when they finally challenge him to describe his practices he tells them how he is able to free himself of all desires, how he exhausts all likes and dislikes, and how he abandons fancy or aversion for talk, which he describes as an echo in a deserted valley. His practices require imaging and meditation; they are by heart and not by mouth, and he is not trapped by mere conceptualization of

2. Ibid., 536.
3. Ibid., 374.

MILAREPA ON DETACHMENT AND WORLDLINESS

the Void. His practices are devoid of a desire for fame. Three more scholar-priests are sent to challenge him and Milarepa targets their jealousy of him: "Correct understanding and merit can only grow from within, otherwise you will be driven in the Miserable Realms by jealousy."[4] His "logic" is practice and merits—fruitful things such as "diligence and perseverance, of remaining in solitude, of meditating in the hermitage, of producing the Realizations and true understanding within."[5] Milarepa smiles when one of the scholars throws a handful of earth at his face, admonishing Milarepa for not answering his questions with scholastic language in Buddhist terms, saying that anyone can sing such "trash." Further challenges by the scholar-priests induce Milarepa's direct reply:

> What is the use of joining the Order?
> If the poisonous snake of Klesa is not killed,
> The yearning for wisdom only leads to fallacy.
> If venomous jealousy is not overcome,
> One's yearning for Bodhi-Mind will be an illusion.
> If one refrains not from hurting people,
> His longing for respect and honor
> Is merely wishful thinking.[6]

"The poisonous snake of Klesa"—greed, hate envy, pride and blindness—is the reason for attachments, and is usually connected with pursuing respect and honor, name and fame. For example, because of pride we hide our anger so that we impress others with our superiority, however false, in order to attract people's good opinions of us.

Milarepa is eventually declared winner of the debate, and one of the logicians contrasts him to the logicians: "We logicians have little sincerity, faith, or devotion; nor do we have the pure thoughts and spirit of renunciation."[7]

It strikes an echo in us when Rechungpa, Milarepa's heart-son, whose attraction to worldliness is evident throughout the songs, is displeased with Milarepa's victory over the logicians, wishing that he had answered in a scholarly manner; when Rechungpa intends to repair this by going to India to learn logic and science in order to beat the scholars; and eventually when he is persuaded by Milarepa to abandon his plan and undertake to obtain

4. Ibid., 380.
5. Ibid., 380.
6. Ibid., 388.
7. Ibid., 374.

teachings of the lineage. This is the same Rechungpa who only a while ago had sung about living with his guru, describing his experience with him as powerful as a sharp knife, cutting inner and outer deception; who when roaming from country to country felt as if he were a tiger, a cub, or a bee:

> Non-attached to all and utterly free,
> because of this, I am happy and gay!
> When I mingled with people in the street,
> I felt as if I were an immaculate lotus
> Standing above all filth and mud.
> Because of this, I am happy and gay!
> When I sat among crowds in the town,
> felt as if I were like rolling mercury—
> It touches all but adheres to nought.
> Because of this, I feel happy and gay![8]

Milarepa suspects that Rechungpa's experiences are motivated by pride, and as we see later these suspicious are not without foundation. Rechungpa evidently longs to mingle with the world as well as be inspired by his guru.

We recognize Rechungpa's struggles as our own: his painstaking steps to shed his old self and to let go of his ambition, his faith in Milarepa, and on the other hand his identification with the world's opposition to the spirit. We understand Rechungpa when he says:

> Though the best guru is one's own mind,
> We need a teacher to illustrate our Mind-Essence.[9]

And also:

> Pray at all times look after this, your son,
> Who has no kinsmen and no friend.
> Pray conquer all his hindrances
> And save him from going astray![10]

Milarepa's arduous journey from his early life when he practiced black magic to his mature years of practicing the wisdom of the Void—realizing through experience that the world is an enemy of the spirit and that no spiritual progress is free from attack by those who pursue worldliness—and his trials with tormenting interior distractions have made him a legitimate authority on spiritual struggles. He is familiar as the untiring spiritual

---

8. Ibid., 436.
9. Ibid., 439.
10. Ibid., 399.

MILAREPA ON DETACHMENT AND WORLDLINESS

director who patiently and with detachment reflects on Rechungpa's desires as distractions from achieving the true goal, "the immaculate Fruit of Nakedness." When Rechungpa returns from India Milarepa warns him:

> You went to India for the Pith-Instructions
> But have brought back books full of arguments.
> You were thus exposed to the danger
> of becoming a debater.
> You wanted to be a yogi,
> but books like those and their ideas
> Could make you a pompous teacher![11]

This solitary and unconventional Buddhist saint and his rebellious heart-son could easily be transported to the twentieth century and hold the interest of those of us who are experiencing conflicts between values of the culture and our own internal values, between highest and strongest values; for instance, between pursuing a career we believe will deliver prestige or money and doing what we love and remaining invisible, or between aspiration and commitment to fulfill the potential of our true self and the pull of the compliant self—such as confronting our boss and acquiring self-respect, though it might cost us our job.

As a Buddhist, Milarepa does not flinch from taking a hard look at the world, at suffering and its causes, with the emphasis on calling the world's bluff. The world promises but does not deliver; it may seem pleasing but it is deceptive; people are easily entrapped by apparently rewarding objects, such as money and property, which once acquired cause fear of loss, and sweet words between relatives and friends, which eventually turn sour. Milarepa looks squarely at the attachments that worldliness induces. Attachments come from ignorance, from being blind to the illusory quality of the benefits that worldliness provides. Suffering lies in attachments, not in the objects of attachments.

Milarepa does not attempt to find ways of alleviating the resulting disappointment, the fear and the grief; he aims at eliminating desire:

> How foolish to spend your lifetime without meaning,
> When a precious human body is so rare a gift.
> How ridiculous to cling to prison-like
> cities and remain there.
> How laughable to fight and quarrel with your
> wives and relatives, who do but visit you.

11. Ibid., 452.

> How senseless to cherish sweet and tender words
> Which are but empty echoes in a dream.
> How silly to disregard one's life fighting foes
> Who are but frail flowers.
>
> How foolish it is when dying to torment
> oneself with thoughts of family,
> Which bind one to Maya's mansion.
> How stupid to stint on property and money,
> Which are a debt on loan from others.
> How ridiculous it is to beautify and deck the body,
> Which is a vessel full of filth.
> How silly to strain each nerve for wealth and goods,
> and neglect the nectar of inner teachings.[12]

We agree it is foolish to neglect inner teachings, but can we see the body as a "vessel full of filth"? And yet this perception brings to mind what a beautiful body can and cannot do for you. It brings to mind what the world can and cannot do for you. It also brings to mind how often we lack perspective when we worry and fret over anticipating future events, and agonize over making decisions, however insignificant.

Milarepa certainly knows how the world affects us negatively. He escapes the villagers, who cling to property, family, money, their bodies, and companionship:

> If one stays too long with friends,
> They will soon tire of him;
> Living in such closeness leads to dislike and hate.
> It is but human to expect and demand too much
> When one dwells too long in companionship.[13]

At one point he retreats to reside alone in the Great Cave of Conquering Demons. There in the utter solitude of the Snow Mountain he tells the villagers who come to visit him and are impressed with his vitality that his battles with forces of nature make him the true successor of his lineage. Mastering his mind injects him with new insights into the frivolity and meaninglessness of clinging to material things:

---

12. Ibid., 33–34.
13. Ibid., 34.

MILAREPA ON DETACHMENT AND WORLDLINESS

> Wealth, at first leads to self-enjoyment,
> Making other people envious.
> However much one has, one never feels it is enough,
> Until one is bound by the miser's demon;
> It is then hard to spend on virtuous deeds.[14]

To rid oneself of desire one must tame one's mind; this is a concept familiar to us. The mind, described as a "whirling vortex" or a nimble bird that now flies high and now swoops low, thinks too much, doesn't devote itself to the practice, and plays tricks on us. It perceives reality incorrectly, endowing it with allure—hence the ego clings to it. The ego-free mind, on the other hand, is indifferent to worldly allure and to the customary perception of reality, its properties and its values, permitting Milarepa to sit "with his penis freely exposed," to the horror of his patrons, to whom he exclaims, "What need have I to follow your customs? Bodhi is spontaneity itself!"[15]

Further descriptions of this indifferent mind leap at us throughout the songs. We hear about the dualistic-knot–free mind that has no substance; the mind that is void, encompassing non-clinging and non-attachment, as well as having no hope, no fear, and no confusion; the mind "where subject and object are one ... When acting and actor disappear."[16] This mind is free of the distinctions of good and evil in all their shadings, and is the mark of deep renunciation:

> If a deep renunciation has
> Not yet arisen in your heart
> Your actionless actions are
> Still bound by hopes and fears.
> Virtuous deeds turn into vices if
> You know not [what is] beyond rejection and
> Acceptance.[17]

The mind that goes beyond distinctions is the "original" mind, the plain, "natural, spontaneous, straightforward, and naked mind"[18] that somehow became polluted with attachments to existence, stained with greed, envy, delusion, pride, and aversion. It is a mind that searches for nothing, that is at ease and relaxed, and that lets go. Interestingly, this

---

14. Ibid., 122.
15. Ibid., 579.
16. Ibid., 29.
17. Ibid., 526.
18. Ibid., 540.

mind that is "completely relaxed" is powerful and strong, indicating the perseverance and determination that the practice of the view brings about. When distracted it has the power to revert to its natural state through the help of its own inner resources:

> The nature of the mind is two-in-one;
> If one discriminates or sees opposites,
> It is one's attachment and affection . . .
> The Essence of Mind is like the sky;
> Sometimes it is shadowed by the clouds
> of Thought-flow.
> Then the wind of the Guru's inner teaching
> Blows away the drifting clouds.[19]

Milarepa's approach to the world—extinguishing the fire of desire in all matters, renouncing all of the world's goods as well as ego attachments to the world (applying his precept in a universal context)—presents difficulties for us. We cannot imagine a desireless, ego-free approach to the world in which there is no distinction between likes and dislikes, rejection and acceptance. It is even more difficult to believe that the world is an illusion, a "shadow-show." We see desire as an integral part of human nature. We place great value on love and seldom think of it without thinking of attachment; we feel that being detached from a beloved means that we do not love. And though love is often the ambassador of loss, grief, and suffering, we remain attached to the object of love. (Alterocentric love, which is detached from the ego and its desires and wants only what is best for the beloved, we practice only on occasion.) We fear losing our attachments to objects and of course losing the objects themselves. Our attachments are familiar to us; they affirm our sense of identity, our patterns of thinking, acting, and feeling about ourselves. However, they erect a barrier against making our unconscious conscious, against the spontaneity that may emerge if we give them up and the unpredictable outcome.

In addition, we who live in the world know of its rewards as well as its sufferings. We know of healthy friendships and healthy family lives. We know the beauty that exists in the world—the beauty in art, literature, and architecture, in the natural love between mother and child, and in erotic love. We attempt to apply concepts to different contexts, insisting that some things are worth desiring and attaining, and some bring us pleasure and joy. We learn to accept our limitations and the limitations of the world. And we

19. Ibid., 133.

acquire resources to deal with a world that is often hostile. Yet Milarepa's songs induce us to be wary of desired things that cause us harm, and they present the possibility in which we can begin to sense freedom, a rewarding result of letting go of liking and disliking, hope and fear, acceptance and rejection; in this respect we transcend the ego and the world. Think of those rare moments when we remain unimpressed with ourselves when praised and don't devalue ourselves when insulted.

In light of Milarepa's experiences we are moved to process our own, and rather than remove ourselves from the world we may work through our attachments and detachments, healthy detachments and unhealthy detachments, in their spiritual and psychological meanings. Healthy detachment does not always entail actually giving up a relationship or an object, but rather having the capacity to let it go when it interferes with something better or when it leaves of its own accord. It is not withdrawal, avoidance, rejection, or aversion. It may entail recognizing the value of the object and seeing how one enjoys it more when one is not clinging to it. It is a "take it or leave it" attitude, with the prospect of a rewarding future. It implies freedom from striving for security. It can bring on a "dark night of the soul"—discouragement, depression, and aridity—a particularly difficult stage, which may feel like a deterioration but is actually a sign of progress.

Milarepa is playful and spontaneous. There is no coercion in any of his teachings. "This is my advice: take it or not," he says, "it is entirely up to you."[20] Even while admonishing his devotees he remains detached from their plight. He sings to an audience but also to himself. His renunciation results in no worry, no fear, no exhaustion, no need to please patrons, no need to prepare for anything, and ultimately in happiness.

In the hands of Milarepa every bit of worldliness and attachment is stripped naked and shown as a cause of suffering. His view is an antidote to the idolatry of the world, which is often all to some people. It cuts through all aspects of the world, including virtues, the monastic life, the scholarly life, and existence itself, bad or good (the dualistic knot), and exposes it as transient, not worth desiring. When we read Milarepa we, like his listeners, are disarmed by his direct and unpretentious manner, and we feel the intensity of our worldly valuations diminish.

---

20. Ibid., 630.

6

SUBTLETIES OF THE SPIRIT[1]

> *"Unknown to me, my king, thou didst press the signet of eternity upon many a fleeting moment of my life."*[2]

IN BIOLOGICAL TERMS WE may think of the mortal psyche as giving birth to and as the mother of the spirit. The psyche is tied to its nest. The spirit, however, uses the nest—the world—without being tied to it. It abandons it as soon as it grows wings. Though not *of* the world, the spirit is *in* the world as an observer, discriminating to discover the essence of everything.

The spiritual life is not compensation for a failed love relationship or for a cultural deprivation, or an escape from a disappointment in the return on investments in the world. It is rather, as the philosopher Santayana says, "the flower of all satisfactions, in which satisfaction becomes free from care, selfless, wholly actual and, in that inward sense, eternal."[3]

There are many misconceptions concerning the spiritual life—notions that connect it with goodness, or with faith, or with holding certain values and virtues sacred. The most common one is confusing the spiritual life with the religious life. The psychoanalyst and philosopher Dr. Preston McLean disentangles this confusion by distinguishing between the two. He characterizes religion as having to do with "housekeeping and bookkeeping," an attachment to prescribed beliefs and to a prescribed way of life, as distinct from the spirit, which breaks through the confinement of its religious environment or any other institutional environment. McLean stresses that the spirit is not bent on results. Pressure to adhere to any belief makes it weary. It lives as a gypsy. Its home is where it is. According to Santayana, "the homelessness of spirit comes from detachment, detachment no

---

1. Originally published online in *Miranda Literary Magazine*, 2009.
2. Tagore, "Gitanjali," 16.
3. Santayana, *Platonism*, 29.

SUBTLETIES OF THE SPIRIT

less from the grander thing which the snob respects and pretends to know as from this humbler thing which he despises."[4]

Often the practice of religion is the basis for the development of the spirit. Though distinct from religion, the spirit *is* influenced by religious values—moral and ethical values and virtues such as truth, courage, and justice. The spirit is impartial and is open to values from all great religions, believing, as Ralph Waldo Emerson says, "in the perpetual openness of the human mind to new influx of light."[5] One can be both religious and spiritual, and great religious personalities noted for their spirituality excel in their ability to renounce immaterial as well as material values. The function of spirit, according to Santayana, is to disintoxicate itself from the influence of *all* values—material, moral, ethical, as well as aesthetic. As it matures, the spirit sees them as they are: relative, transient, inevitable, although useful for the purpose of transcending them. When the spirit grows out of these values it leaves them behind in order to live its own form of life—free and detached.

St. Teresa of Avila is a paradigm of moving effortlessly between the religious life and the spiritual life. Having seen the laxity of spiritual practices in the existing Carmelite convents, she actively pursues the building of new, reformed convents. She is life affirming, engaging with the world—even with the political world, negotiating with the highest civil and religious authorities—to achieve her goal. She thus exhibits a penchant for the religious life that is concerned with housekeeping and bookkeeping. But St. Teresa is also life denying and world denying, aiming to renounce whatever she thinks would interfere with the soul uniting with God. This includes any form of social contact in the convent. The evolution of her own spiritual life involves developing skills for detaching more completely from everything that is worldly, everything that is not God.

Gandhi too renounces everything that is not God—that is, not Truth. He adheres to Hindu religious practices such as not eating meat and setting time for regular prayer. He is also religious in the sense of being tied to the results of his leadership of the non-violent resistance to British rule. But most significantly he renounces possessions, sex, and aggression of any kind, which he sees as interfering with the realization of Truth. He subtitles his autobiography *The Story of My Experiments with Truth*—the truth of renunciation. Gandhi worships God as Truth only, and for him God alone is real.

4. Ibid., 53.
5. Emerson, *Essays*, 90.

PSYCHE, SOUL, AND SPIRIT

One of the fruits of renouncing the world, and existence itself—a renunciation that is hearty and radical—is, according to Santayana, a universal love of nature, "a love unqualified by prejudice, by envy, by fear of being outshone or discountenanced by the marvels which nature or society may elsewhere bring to light."[6] Mother Teresa, who devotes her life to the care of dying poor people, when asked, "What's your secret?" replies, "I want nothing."

A hearty renunciation of the ego and the body is apparent in the life and teachings of the Hindu sage Sri Ramana Maharshi. The Maharshi doesn't identify with his ego or his body, feelings, or thoughts. When he contracts cancer he is aware of the pain but doesn't identify with it. He doesn't resist it but rather surrenders to it. "Occasionally he would admit 'there is pain' but he would never say 'I have pain.'"[7] The Maharshi does not attempt to stop the pain, nor does he struggle to understand the reason for the pain; he just asks to let things take their course. "There is no cause for alarm. The body itself is a disease; let it have its natural end."[8] He yields to the cyclical nature of things, the process of growth and decay—the loss of youth, health, and life, and the daily occurrences of physical and emotional pain, as well as joy.

From the Maharshi's point of view there are no disciples; all are enlightened, all are one with him. He insists on being treated as not different from anyone. His disciples experience his grace, which is like an ocean, as Osborne puts it, in which each dips his vessel, large or small, according to his choice. The Maharshi embodies the spirit that Santayana describes as dwelling in the infinite, the "indestructible and inevitable infinite that contains everything, but contains it only in its essence, in that eternal quality of being in which everything is a companion and supplement to everything else, never a rival or a contradiction."[9] On this last subject McLean once remarked that if we were to "de-siblingize" the world we would live in Paradise.

The eternal quality of being is what the poet Rainer Maria Rilke calls "that first home": a state of being where one is free of death, where the animal who "has its decline in back of it, forever, and God in front, [and when it moves it] moves already in eternity, like a fountain," and in whose face we see "the Open," a life that is "boundless, unfathomable ... pure like

---

6. Ibid., 92–93.
7. Osborne, *Maharshi*, 182.
8. Ibid., 180.
9. Santayana, *Platonism*, 67.

SUBTLETIES OF THE SPIRIT

its outward gaze."[10] It is a state of being where worldly values such as name and fame, power and money are seen as illusions, objects for contempt, because they don't deliver the promised satisfactions; a state of being that according to Santayana is indifferent to anything that it might miss—it is not impatient with one thing and longing for another: "what it possesses it cannot lose; what it leaves out is not denied or condemned or demanded."[11] It is a state of being where one is not concerned about being shunned or ignored by the world, and is dismissive of the insults that the world heaps on it—a world that labels the spiritual person idealistic, unrealistic, blind, naïve, and the like.

Tagore writes about such a person who is on a journey with friends, searching for God. The friends race ahead, whereas he, noticing a shepherd boy who "drowsed and dreamed in the shadow of the banyan tree,"[12] lies down by the water and stretches his tired limbs on the grass, joining the boy in simply being. This person is not only dismissive of the world and the world's aim but is glad to be attacked by the world: "My companions laughed at me in scorn; . . . Mockery and reproach pricked me to rise, but found no response in me. I gave myself up for lost in the depth of a glad humiliation."[13] This "glad humiliation," so foreign to a worldly way of thinking, is one of the radical hallmarks of a spiritual person. He welcomes the scorn as proof that he is on the right path; more importantly, he is glad for the opportunity to grow in humility.

In the Sermon on the Mount Jesus elevates the lowly to an exalted status, along with the ones who mourn, those who are persecuted, those who "hunger and thirst" for righteousness, the merciful, and the pure in heart. They are the ones who are blessed; who will be strengthened, comforted, satisfied; who will see God. Tagore is attuned to the place the lowly hold in God's heart: "I was singing all alone in a corner, and the melody caught your ear. . . . One plaintive little strain mingled with the great music of the world, and with a flower for a prize you came down and stopped at my cottage door."[14]

Disenchantment, even with the finer things such as learning and culture, and then re-enchantment with ordinary and humble objects that

---

10. Rilke, "Eighth Elegy," 193.
11. Santayana, *Platonism*, 75.
12. Tagore, "Gitanjali," 18.
13. Ibid.
14. Ibid., 19.

the world ignores, are implied in Hugo von Hofmannsthal's "The Lord Chandos Letter." The writer exhibits qualities of the artist, who, according to Santayana, "lives only in his own labor, irresponsible, technical, and visionary."[15] Hofmannsthal is thrilled in the presence of the infinite that he sees in "the half-filled watering can left under a walnut tree,"[16] exalted by what to most people is a wretched thing not worthy of notice. To him the watering can is an eternal possession: "even the most abject creature . . . a rat, a water bug, a gnarled apple tree . . . becomes more to me than the loveliest, most yielding partner ever was in my night of intensest passion."[17] Hofmannsthal would rather gaze at "far-off, solitary shepherd's fire" than at the "starry firmament,"[18] and he would more likely be in rapture from "the chirping from one last dying cricket . . . than from the majestic roar of an organ."[19] When he talks about the objects under the tree, "a juxtaposition of trifles," he experiences a thrill that might have caused him to call down "the very cherubim in which I do not believe," and he turns away from that spot every time he goes by there in order not to disturb "the aftersense of the miraculous still wafting there about its trunk."[20]

William Carlos Williams' poem "The Red Wheelbarrow" also calls our attention to an ordinary object: "So much depends / upon / a red wheel / barrow / glazed with rain / water / beside the white / chickens."[21] "So much depends" represents the way the wheelbarrow evokes the experience of transcending its primary and secondary qualities—the colors, the shape, and the wetness. This is an experience of eternal time intervening in temporal time. Spurred by imagination, exalted by the rhythm of his poem, and freeing himself from sensual attachment to the wheelbarrow, Williams mentions in a conversation that he was refining and clarifying and intensifying "that eternal moment in which we alone live."[22] Williams writes about ordinary things and then, as Louis Simpson says, strives to "lift into perfection, the Nirvana of art."[23]

15. Santayana, *Platonism*, 40.
16. Hofmannsthal, *Lord Chandos*, 26.
17. Ibid., 26–27.
18. Ibid., 29.
19. Ibid., 29–30.
20. Ibid., 26.
21. Williams, "Wheelbarrow," 292.
22. Ellman, *Norton*, 286.
23. Simpson, *Tower*, 268.

SUBTLETIES OF THE SPIRIT

How infinity is related to our lives is a pressing question to Rilke:

> Does the infinite space
> we dissolve into, taste of us then? Do the angels really
> reabsorb only the radiance that streamed out from themselves, or
> of our essence in it as well?[24]

A related sensibility, regarding how love preserves the object of love forever, is expressed in another elegy by Rilke:

> I know,
> you touch so blissfully because the caress preserves,
> because the place you so tenderly cover
> does not vanish; because underneath it
> you feel pure duration.[25]

To penetrate the nature of spirituality, Par Lagerkvist, in his story "The Basement," describes a beggar who, like Tagore, is all alone and "singing." The narrator has seen Lindgren on the street, the little old man with the withered legs, lowly and suffering. He feels that he has something to learn from the beggar. He befriends Lindgren, who invites him to his apartment in the basement. The narrator discovers with surprise that the apartment is well taken care of, and there was something warm and secure about him, "not as he was in the street." The beggar eats his meal of coffee and a piece of bread with reverence and tranquility. His face is radiant; he is obviously content and grateful for what he has, and is not living in misery as expected, unlike the narrator, who lives "the real life" and has no peace. It leaves the narrator both moved and depressed, and thinking that there must be something that Lindgren hopes for. Does Lindgren believe in a prevailing God who has a higher purpose in the afflictions he has given him? "'No,' he replied slowly, 'not when one's life can be like mine.'"[26] Lindgren feels that his life is full, albeit "each day is heavy to bear." To him a "rich and glorious" life is an interior, contented life. The life of poverty and hardship, which has stripped Lindgren down to essentials, turns out to be a life that outlasts and outshines other lives; the narrator says, "The old man's lamp lighted me nearly all the way home."[27]

---

24. Rilke, "Second Elegy," 157.
25. Ibid., 159.
26. Lagerkvist, "Basement," 71.
27. Ibid.

PSYCHE, SOUL, AND SPIRIT

The Sufi Bishr Ibn el-Harith tells a similar story of finding spiritual riches in a life of apparent misery. The Sufi sees a blind leper lying on the ground alone. He comforts the leper, speaking some words of reassurance out of his sorrow and compassion. The leper responds, "'What stranger comes here, to stand between me and my Lord? With or without my body, I have my love for Him.'"[28] It is a lesson the Sufi never forgets.

The spirit, embodied by the saint and the artist alike, is, in the view of Rilke, tender and open and participates in the wretchedness of lives. The leper is a symbol for wretchedness. In *Letters on Cezanne* Rilke discusses the artist's life with respect to the self-overcoming exhibited in "lying-down-with-the-leper and sharing all one's warmth with him."[29] This "self-overcoming" is not limited to experience with people, but includes the artist's depiction of objects in their essences without interjecting the self. Rilke characterizes the artists Chardin and Cezanne as leading the way. He points out that Chardin stripped the eighteenth-century blue of its pretension and that Cezanne went further and used it without a secondary significance, as pure color. In Chardin the fruits are scattered on the table, no longer carefully arranged for a fancy meal. In Cezanne the fruits "cease to be edible altogether, that's how thinglike and real they become, how simply indestructible in their stubborn thereness."[30] These painters love the objects as they are making them, but do not show that love in the paintings, thus removing their feelings and allowing the pure essence of the objects to emerge, untainted.

A kinship with and delight in all things natural is at the heart of traditional Haiku. The poet Issa sees a snail as a fellow being:

> Where can he be going
> In the rain,
> This snail?[31]

Another Haiku by Issa expresses his intuitive unintellectual response to a flower:

> Just simply alive,
> Both of us, I

---

28. Shah, *Sufi*, 209.
29. Rilke, *Cezanne*, 68.
30. Ibid., 33.
31. Blyth, *Haiku*, 3:247.

SUBTLETIES OF THE SPIRIT

And the poppy.[32]

In the phrase "simply alive" one senses a dropping away of everything that impacts us. "Simply alive" is a statement of beingness, contentment, acceptance of what simply is. "Both of us" indicates that the poet and the poppy are united.

In other Haiku the poets respond to tiny and humble events, each of which is a distillation of natural life. Shiki writes:

> The sparrow hops
> along the verandah,
> with wet feet.[33]

We can see the footprints of the sparrow. Basho writes:

> The old pond:
> A frog jumps in, —
> The sound of the water.[34]

We can hear the plop. Another Haiku by Basho envelopes us with a fragrance not described:

> I don't know
> which tree it comes from,
> that fragrance.[35]

The sparrow leaving footprints on the verandah, the frog making a sound when jumping in the pond, the flowering tree emitting the fragrance; all these, though transient, are not lost. Their essences seem to visit from eternity.

Haiku and the other quoted poems are examples of a spontaneous loving response to the things that are before us. Santayana notes, "It is of the essence of spirit to see and love things for their own sake, in their own nature, not for the sake of one another, not for *its* own sake."[36] The thing is loved not because it is recommended or required to love it, or because it is in fashion to love it, but because it is lovely as we see it now in our fresh, open, and unattached way. We may not have loved it in the past, and we

---

32. Blyth, *Haiku*, 4:xxvi.
33. Blyth, *Haiku*, 2:234.
34. Ibid., 2:253.
35. Hass, *Haiku*, 21.
36. Santayana, *Platonism*, 93.

may not always love it. We see this aspect of spirit, as the Maharshi points out, in the child and the sage in that they both are interested in incidents only as long as they last. Tagore writes, "Children have their play on the seashore of worlds. They know not how to swim, they know not how to cast nets. Pearl-fishers dive for pearls, merchants sail in their ships, while children gather pebbles and scatter them again."[37]

---

37. Tagore, "Crescent Moon," 41–42.

7
JEREMIAH: CREATIVE ADVANCE[1]

JEREMIAH CRIES OUT TO God that God's word has brought him "insult, and derision, all day long," and that he has determined not to think about God; but "there seemed to be a fire burning in my heart imprisoned in my bones," which he cannot not restrain.[2] Thus transmitting God's word to the Israelites has become Jeremiah's life's work, and along with his life it represents guidance for personal growth and a reminder of the need for social justice. Many useful concepts, such as deception, a new heart, social reform, surrender of self, the value of exile, and enduring and paying the cost of conviction and commitment, are part of his story.

Jeremiah is sent by God, in the sixth century BC, to save the Israelites from total destruction by the Babylonians, who are about to descend on Judah. Knowing that the Israelites cannot defeat the powerful army of the enemy, he calls on them to surrender and go into exile in Babylon, thus surrendering to the word of God. The relationship between the Jews and God, and their existence as a people, depends upon their obedience to God. Procrastination and defiance notwithstanding, the Israelites, from their very beginnings as a nation in the desert, on hearing God's commandments declare, "We shall observe, and obey."

This people's special relationship to God does not hold unless they cease their habitual straying and unite with their God, his Law, and his word. In Jeremiah's time, the temple, intended to be the crown of religious experience, has become the locale of deception. It does not fulfill God's purpose; moreover, with worship being insincere, the temple is antithetical to its purpose. The city is bogged down in the material world. Worship needs only prayers and obedience to God's word; the rest is window dressing.

---

1. Originally published in Hebrew in *Eretz Acheret* 22 (June–July 2004) 82–85. Translated by Yaniv Farkash.

2. Jer 20:9. All biblical quotations in this essay are from the Jerusalem Bible.

PSYCHE, SOUL, AND SPIRIT

Jeremiah admonishes the people in the name of God: "What do I care about incense imported from Sheba, or fragrant cane from a distant country? Your holocausts are not acceptable, your sacrifices do not please me."[3] Among the acts that please God is a concern for social justice, which is part of his being: "It is He who sees justice done for the orphan and widow, who loves the stranger and gives him food and clothing."[4] Jeremiah calls for spiritual reform, which, in its emphasis on a new heart, speaks to the overruling value in Judaism, justice, and its offspring, social justice. The call for reform embraces the need for action that will include supporting those who lack the power to care for themselves. Jeremiah, passionate about justice, is appalled by social inequality and by the exploiters of the helpless: "in wickedness they go to any lengths, they have no respect for rights, for orphans' rights, to support them, they do not uphold the cause of the poor."[5] Jeremiah speaks to the people on behalf of God, but he is also the advocate of the people, pleading with God to protect them, reminding God that the course of humankind is not in their own control.[6]

For Jeremiah spiritual life overflows into the religious active life. However, a sincere heart and compassionate conduct being difficult to achieve, the people rely on superficial religious behavior to curry the favor of God. While they consistently repudiate the Law, worshipping other gods and disregarding social justice, they wallow in self-deception by claiming to possess the Law. The people abandon the vital element of compassion in their religious and spiritual practice, not only neglecting but exploiting the needy for material gain, and deceiving themselves, and perhaps thinking they can deceive God, that their rituals of worship are sufficient to fulfill God's will. Their self-deception has serious consequences that reach beyond damage to the self: it blinds them to the suffering of others, diminishing their own humanity as they dismiss the value of the others. Having turned their back on God, they have caused the loss of the nation's spiritual core, opening the way for decay. Participating physically in God's experience of anger and grief, Jeremiah follows his instructions to bury his loincloth, which clings to his body as Israel is supposed to cling to God; later God tells him to dig it up, and he finds the loincloth rotting. God then says to Jeremiah that he will rot away the pride of Judah and Jerusalem for following *their* desires,

3. Jer 6:20.
4. Deut 10:18.
5. Jer 5:28.
6. Jer 10:23.

JEREMIAH: CREATIVE ADVANCE

worshipping other gods, and defeating God's purpose, who created them to be *his* people.[7]

Jeremiah exposes the deceit of those in power "who spread their nets; like fowlers they set snares, but it is men they catch. Like a cage full of birds so are their houses full of loot; they have grown rich and powerful because of it, fat and sleek."[8] He excoriates King Jehoiakim for living luxuriously on the backs of oppressed laborers, for having concern for nothing but his own interest. The same self-interest and the desire for short-lived comforts is evident in the episode of the liberated slaves, when the people of Jerusalem make a pact with King Zedekiah to free their slaves and then go back on their word.

The corruption of the people and of the king goes hand in hand with that of the false prophets: "the prophets prophesy falsely, the priests teach whatever they please, and my people love it!"[9] There is complacency, a satisfaction with the status quo. The false prophets tell the people what the people want to hear—that peace will be theirs and no misfortune will touch them. They deny the decay of the religious life along with the reality of the threat of destruction. They deny the fact that peace is hard won. Jeremiah identifies their prophecies as "delusive visions, hollow predictions, day-dreams of their own."[10] This self-deception blinds the false prophets *and* the people to the potential for non-delusional peace contained within the troubles.

To Jeremiah, an Israelite, political surrender is inextricably bound up with a personal/communal one. Personal and communal lives and nationhood interact with the religious life of the Jews and bear the same tone and texture of purpose. Although the objects of surrender that Jeremiah speaks of are different—one is land, belonging to the political, and the other is self-deception and stubbornness, belonging to the personal/communal will—both are concerned with the ultimate purpose of embodying the life of the religion and of the spirit.

The notion of surrendering one's own will is basic to Jeremiah. Blessed with very little egotism to interfere with his "hearing" and emptied of his own will, Jeremiah becomes a vessel for God's word. He exemplifies a complete physical and spiritual surrender, not only uniting with God's word but also identifying with God's suffering over the straying of hs people. This

---

7. Jer 13:18.
8. Jer 5:27–28.
9. Jer 5:31.
10. Jer 14:14.

surrender, and the resultant effect of becoming closer to God, runs through Judaism. Abraham, having been seized by terror in the making of the covenant, becomes completely open and surrenders to what God intends for him and his descendants. Moses, facing the burning bush, in taking off his shoes performs the symbolic act of deference in which he is vulnerable, open to receiving the word of God.

Centuries later the concept of surrender still runs through Judaism, as in Hasidsim, where surrender has to do with the individual and God, focusing on the flaw of egotism. Martin Buber tells a story of a disciple of the Great Maggid who, after having completed instructions by him, decides to visit his friend Rabbi Aaron of Karlin. When he knocks on the lit window and is asked by Rabbi Aaron who it is, the disciple answers "I." Rabbi Aaron does not open the window. Each time the disciple knocks and is asked who it is, he identifies himself as "I." The window remains closed. Exasperated, the disciple asks why Rabbi Aaron does not open, and the answer in a grave voice says, "Who is it that dares call himself 'I' that befits only God himself!"[11] The disciple then knows that he has not learned enough, has not surrendered his egotism, and he returns to the Great Maggid.

The concept of surrender has applications other than religious to our daily lives. In some relationships, such as between spouses or partners, we might need to let go of the urge to dominate. When we expand into new territories of knowledge and experience, we need to relinquish our investment in old beliefs and ideologies, on which we have expended much time and effort, along with the vanity connected with possessing knowledge.

Psychoanalytical literature seldom uses the term *surrender*. One of the exceptions is in the writings of the psychoanalyst Emmanuel Ghent, who introduces this notion in contrast to submission and masochism. In his work, surrender, "rather than carrying a connotation of defeat," instead conveys "a quality of liberation and expansion of the self as a corollary of the letting down of defensive barriers."[12] Ghent believes that surrender indicates some "'force' towards growth," pressing us to discover the true self and break down the false self. The false self is the compliant, submissive self, constructed to protect the true self from insult; it sometimes uses deceptions, such as denials and rationalizations, to protect against "anxiety, shame, guilt, anger."[13] Surrender does not imply surrender to another—that

11. Buber, *Tales*, 1:200.
12. Ghent, "Masochism," 108.
13. Ibid,. 110.

JEREMIAH: CREATIVE ADVANCE

is submission. Surrender in this context is done within the self. It implies letting go of the false self and allows one to discover one's identity. Jeremiah in exhorting the people to surrender to God is passionate for them to return to their true nature as spiritual people.

Jeremiah has enough faith in himself as a messenger of God to endure the attacks and persecutions he suffers from the people of his time. He follows God's orders not to enter any house of the people, whether they are mourning or rejoicing. His derision of a religious practice devoid of spirituality, and insistence on the need for spiritual and religious reform, fulfilling the rights and supporting the needy—orphans, widows, and the poor—coupled with a call to surrender to God's word, create enemies of the priests and the false prophets. He is accused of desertion and of disheartening the soldiers who are defending Jerusalem by telling them to leave the city and surrender to the Chaldeans troops in order to survive. When King Zedekiah throws Jeremiah's written call for surrender into the fire, Jeremiah writes it again and sends it to the king a second time. He establishes his credibility by being willing to die for his vision. (No false prophet is prepared to do that.) He challenges the people who oppose him to do what they will, but if they kill him, he says, "you will be bringing innocent blood on yourselves, on this city and on its citizens."[14] With truth on his side he stands firm.

Jeremiah, however, is no stoic; his surrender to God's word, which burns within him, and his endurance and perseverance are not without bitter complaints, whose concern is threefold: his failure to transform his people, his physical suffering at their hands, and his experiences of God's suffering. He is an example of what it takes to hear God's word and to deliver a harsh message to people whom one loves.

The idea of suffering for God is a dominant theme in Judaism, and appears in Hasidism, which often explores the life of suffering and enduring. Levi Yitzhak of Berditchev pleads to God to show him the meaning of what is happening to him and what it demands of him: "Ah, it is not why I suffer, that I wish to know, but only whether I suffer for your sake."[15] Rabbi Zusya of Hanipol was purported to have not noticed his anguish and needs. He accepted suffering with love.

In spite of the persecutions Jeremiah identifies with himself, not with the enemy. He does not stray from his faith in God and his mission. Job too,

---

14. Jer 26:14–15.
15. Buber, *Tales*, 1:213.

though his circumstances of being tested by God are much different from Jeremiah's, identifies with himself. Having been besieged by the losses of all his children, servants, and possessions, and by the affliction of skin ulcers from head to toe, Job confronts God. He acknowledges God's superiority in the court of justice, for after all God is the judge as well as the defender; nevertheless Job "shall speak, not fearing him." He pleads to God to tell him the reason for his assault and says, "You know very well that I am innocent." He rejects his friends' arguments that he must have sinned and their advice to accept his suffering as correction of or punishment for his sins. Job, far from being submissive to these beliefs, once again challenges God: "Let God answer me.... I will give Him an account of every step of my life, and go as boldly as a prince to meet Him."[16] Ultimately, God's speeches about his all-powerful nature, his acts, and his purposes that humanity cannot know cause Job to retract his arguments. Job realizes that he has been holding on to matters he cannot understand. He repents of trying to understand all God's designs and surrenders his need to do this. He remains identified with himself; his surrender to God comes from having seen God with his own eyes, an opening up tantamount to faith. (The subject of faith, generally the province of religion, has found its way into psychoanalytic literature. In the words of psychoanalyst Michael Eigen, in his discussion of the psychoanalyst Wilfred Bion, "faith involves a radical opening up and letting go. Nothing is held on to, not even love of knowledge."[17])

Jeremiah's purpose is for the people to renew their covenant with God. The covenant requires obedience to the Law based on the religion of a sincere heart—a communal heart and an individual heart. The idea of a new, circumcised heart first appears in Deuteronomy, where God commands the Israelites to write the Law in their hearts. The heart that is engraved by the Law is no longer distracted by idols; it is indestructible.[18] David prays to God to create a clean heart in him and put a new and constant spirit in him.[19] Ezekiel likens the transformation of the heart to a process inspired by God's spirit that turns the obstinate heart of stone to a heart of flesh,[20] issuing in sincerity and respect for the observances.

---

16. Job 31:35–37.
17. Eigen, *Mystic*, 125.
18. Deut 6:7; 10:16.
19. Ps 51:11.
20. Ezek 36:26–27.

JEREMIAH: CREATIVE ADVANCE

Circumcision of the heart has to do with purging the old heart of unjust treatment of the have-nots, worship of idols, and deception: "The heart is more devious than any other thing, perverse too: who can pierce its secrets?"[21] Jeremiah describes the manifestation of this old heart when he castigates the people's moral bankruptcy: "the words they utter are deceitful; 'Peace!' each say to his neighbor, while in his heart plotting a trap for him."[22] In personal relationships this declaration of peace may be to disarm the other, covering up for destructive intentions. It is in contrast to an act of reparation for damage done out of concern for the other, followed by reconciliation, a form of true peace between two people.

The Law, inscribed on the new heart that is open and receptive, will be performed not as a perfunctory act but through an internal stirring. Rituals based on sheer habit, devoid of sincerity, are not a substitute for practicing the essence of the religion, its spirit. Jeremiah's own heart is pure, enabling him to see farther, to hear the truth, to be God's vessel. His mature heart acts "as a faithful flag of warning for troubles ahead."[23] We recall the story told by a Hasidic rabbi who asked the zaddik of Neskhizh whether it was true that he could see and hear all things. The zaddik answered, "Man has been so created to see and hear whatever he wants to. It is only a question of his not corrupting his eyes and his ears."[24]

In giving his young followers advice on purifying their hearts in the worship of God, a Hasidic master recites one of his prayers, which expresses his struggles to overcome impure thoughts and lusts. He says of his heart, "instead of becoming a golden bell whose sound is heard on entering the holy place, the voice of a wicked man is heard in her."[25] He bemoans the coarseness of his soul's heart. His confession is accompanied by a cry to God to purify his soul, remove the evil inclination from him.

Jeremiah exhorts his people to accept exile instead of death at the hands the Babylonians. He has a vision of good figs and bad, symbolizing those who obey God and those who do not. Exile, according to Jeremiah, is a punishment for abandoning God, but also it will save lives. In addition, exile provides a context for self-examination. It is a break in continuity, forcibly keeping people away from physical attachments, from everything

---

21. Jer 17:9.
22. Jer 9:8.
23. Corvan, *Gracian*, 27.
24. Buber, *Tales*, 1:165.
25. Jacobs, *Prayer*, 33.

desired and familiar; it is a catalyst for penitence. As we see in the story of Joseph in Egypt, exile can be a place for finding one's true self and expressing it through creative living. Joseph names his second son Ephraim, a name derived from the Hebrew word for fruitful, "because God has made me fruitful in the country of my misfortune."[26]

Other religions refer to states of individual suffering that resemble exile in their power to facilitate spiritual growth. The Buddhist Bardo, a period of forty-nine days between the moment of death and the moment of rebirth, is a time of intense endurance. It is a place of loss where one examines old habits and thoughts, a time of purification.

Often spiritual suffering is characterized by aridity. St. John of the Cross describes a kind of spiritual exile when he talks of his "dark night of the soul," when one is purged of a delight in the will, when "breasts of the desires and affections of the sensual part of the soul" are dried up and drained.[27] This fertile desert is where emptiness is filled with faith and humiliation of the ego "breeds exaltation."

There is a kind of painful psychological exile. According to the psychoanalyst Melanie Klein, becoming an integrated person means integrating our good (loving, creative) parts and our bad (hating, destructive) parts. Our fear of our destructive parts requires that we split them off, disowning them. It is as if we are in exile from our whole selves. This exile contributes to a feeling of loneliness, which is misunderstood as a feeling of social isolation. Developing a benign, supportive conscience is what we need to help us in this lifelong journey home.

The destruction of the old life that exile entails is a tragedy, yet it contains possibility for creative advance into something new. Psychoanalysis deals with similar processes. Eigen says that what psychoanalysis does is help us incorporate our deformities and disabilities into a "larger rhythm of decimation and flow." In the process of suffering the agonies again and again there is "an opening, a recovery, a movement towards another place."[28]

Whitehead makes the point that understanding that tragedy is not in vain is accompanied by an inner feeling of peace. Peace transcends pain and loss; there is a purification of emotions. Allied to the concept that tragedy contains the seeds of advance is psychoanalyst D. W. Winnicott's concept of the value of depression. The fact of depression indicates that one

---

26. Gen 41:52.
27. John of the Cross, *Dark Night*, 189.
28. Eigen, *Sensitive Self*, 19.

has accepted the feelings of hate. It contains the germ of recovery within it and implies ego strength. If the depression is free of pathological illness the person may come out of a depression "stronger, wiser and more stable" than before. Similarly, in biology a broken bone, after healing, can be stronger than before.

Great religious personalities like Jeremiah who are willing to pay a huge cost for their goals can inspire us and give us perspective about our efforts. They also serve as examples of not flinching from reality. For the spiritual person this means knowing that you will be attacked by people with worldly values; this opposition is proof that one is "going in the right direction," that the suffering is an agent for creative advance.

Jeremiah foresees that exile will have positive results in the future—the people and their heritage will survive. Contrary to common perception, he is not a prophet of doom but a pragmatic prophet who envisions reality. Jeremiah's conception is spontaneous and intuitive, rather than reasoned from experience, but it is pragmatic nevertheless. As he prophesies, the Israelites return to their land seventy years later. In the Maccabean time, four centuries later, the Jews fought the oppressor and did not surrender, nevertheless they revered Jeremiah as a savior of the nation.

8

THOUGHTS ON PSYCHE, SOUL, AND SPIRIT[1]

> ABSTRACT: *There are differences in the meaning and use of the terms* psyche, soul, *and* spirit, *and these differences have large implications for mental health professionals and their clients. For instance, problems of the soul cannot be reduced to symptoms of psychological ill health. Along with pursuing psychological health, one can use religious and spiritual resources in the writings of and about saints and heroes to do the work of spiritual growth.*

"BETWEEN NOW AND THE next session think about your joys and your sorrows." This is how Dr. Preston McLean began therapy with a patient. The patient was struck by the psychoanalyst's attention not to her happiness (which is largely a matter of luck in circumstances in which one was raised) or to her depression, but rather to a deeper part of herself—her soul.

We can understand the meanings of the words *psyche* and *soul* and *spirit* from their uses in our language. (McLean makes a distinction between spirituality and religion, using the word *spirit* in an uncommon way. His characterizations of spirituality and religion are explained later in this essay.) Though we cannot picture the soul or the psyche we feel that they inhabit the body; they are different aspects of interior life. The word *psyche* is not in use in everyday life and is available for understanding mainly in psychological literature. On the other hand, the words *soul* and *spirit* are in common use. We know what we mean when we say "she has soul," or "his credentials are his soul," or "she dances from her soul," "soul food," "soul music," "loses her soul," "sold his soul." These phrases express a sense of authenticity and integrity that we associate with the soul. Sometimes people think in terms of a strong soul and a weak soul, and sometimes we speak of a person with soul or a soulless person. We know what it means when we say "his spirit is low" or "how spiritual she is." In many cases the meaning of a thing cannot be put

---

1. Originally published in the *Journal of Religion and Health* 37/4 (Winter 1998) 313–22.

THOUGHTS ON PSYCHE, SOUL, AND SPIRIT

into words but can only be manifested—in conduct, in the life and works of a person. Socrates manifested his soul in his life and his death.

The word *spirit* was originally connected with breath and the act of breathing, and is associated with aspiration and inspiration. It brings to mind the philosopher Whitehead's concept of God as a lure for feeling and Plato's Ideas as ideals such as goodness, truth, and beauty. The soul or spirit, without losing its sense of what is, is drawn to what ought to be; yearning and searching are words associated with the soul.

Language is about forms of life. A form of life associated with the soul or spirit includes spending time on understanding and implementing values such as goodness, truth, and beauty—contemplating the beauty of a blossom or the lives of saints who would rather lose their lives than lose their souls. This form of life of the soul includes moments when one is deeply moved by altruistic love and compassion, feeling sorrow for damage done in fantasy or in fact by oneself or by others. The soul says "I won't do that," but it fears it might do that under torture and betray itself or others. The soul mourns what could have been, but was not. It has the potential to repair, to restore, to renew, to remedy, to amend a wrong done, to save. The soul aims to mend character; it speculates and imagines; it is visionary; it is illuminated by possibility; it enlarges one's horizon and connects one to the world around, embracing it warmly without possessing it.

The soul is stirred by things ordinary and by things holy. The senses support the life of the soul, yet they sometimes interfere with it. The biblical tribe of priests who served in the holy of holies had to fulfill their tasks in such away that they neither touched nor saw the holy things that they carried, lest they die—a way of preserving what belongs to God, or a way of protecting the concept of God. Similarly, when God identified himself speaking from the burning bush, Moses, afraid to look at God, covered his face.

The words *soul* and *psyche* have an historical connection. Socrates discovered the soul. In the dialogue "Apology" he characterizes his teaching as a single-minded pursuit to persuade people to care about the improvement of their soul and not about their possessions or their personal advancement. Before Socrates Athenians thought of the *psyche*, the Greek word for soul, as a non-material "copy" of the body; Socrates gave the word a spiritual dimension. The meaning of the word *soul* has since evolved from its use in the fields of philosophy, religion, spirituality, esthetics, literature, and even biology, according to some biologists.

PSYCHE, SOUL, AND SPIRIT

The meaning of the word *psyche* has evolved from its use in the fields of psychology, psychoanalysis, and psychiatry. Winnicott points out that the development of the psyche depends on remembering the past, being aware of the present, anticipating the future, and tying them together. The psyche makes sense of our sense of self; it has a capacity to create, to choose, to refuse to adapt, to perceive external reality, and to go further than environmental influences can explain. However, this characterization of the psyche lacks the spiritual and emotional richness and the extra value that come to mind when we think of the soul. For example, the motivation to change oneself that arises in the psyche differs from the motivation that arises in the soul; one may desire to diminish one's anger for the sake of improving one's interpersonal relationships, whereas if one lives from the soul one would be motivated to remove the anger for its own sake or because it is damaging to oneself and others.

The soul has a religious dimension and a spiritual dimension; distinctions between these two are made by McLean. One's religion is what one believes and what one does with the purpose of securing and promoting results, home, future, repose, and rest. (A person's religion may or may not have the view and practice of a particular organized religion.) When the word *religion* is used in this broad sense, we can see religion in the doctor's or the homemaker's daily work. The religious doctor makes rounds in the hospital and keeps records of her or his patients. She or he relies on records and regular examinations of the patient for the purpose of curing the patient. The religious homemaker cleans the house and does the shopping and the cooking. He or she aims to nurture and please the family. Both are bent on results. These activities involve being tied or bound to something (the Latin word for *bind* is the root word of *religion*). The homemaker may discover, however, that he or she is unconsciously interested in curing people, or the doctor in homemaking. The soul, insofar as its interest is religion, concerns itself with concepts of virtues and sins that promote goodness and eradicate or neutralize evil.

In contrast to the religious aspect of the soul, the spiritual aspect—the spirit (not in its common usage)—wanders and is at home wherever it is, reposes and rests in whatever it is contemplating, and is result free and future free. The spirit is complete; it does not possess, hold, or grab; it is open to love, embracing the alien, the unattractive, the "adulterous woman," the sinner, the sick, and the dying. The spirit transcends time; it is not concerned with temporal time, but with eternal time, which intervenes in temporal time. An example is the beauty expressed in music, dance, and art.

The spiritual self benefits the environment but without the motivation to do so, which is the motivation of the religious self. For example, the spiritual psychotherapist, when in a session with a patient, is detached from the desire that the patient make progress; he or she attends, listens, and speaks the patient's language.

The spirit is not entangled with the world, and the world is hostile to the spirit. Santayana points out that the spirit submits to the limitations imposed by the world, but it does experience them as limitations. The territory of the spirit is an eternal world stirred by inwardness.

Jesus, though he came to save the world, would have continued with his mission as a fisher of men even if he had saved not one soul. Milarepa sometimes sang to people in order to convert them, but he often sang to himself songs of self-realization and renunciation alone in his cave, not being concerned with proving himself. It is interesting that the root of the word *prove* is probare, meaning to test a thing for its goodness, to try, to approve, to make good; acts of these great religious personalities came out of concern and not from the desire to be proved or be approved by the world.

When Socrates is sentenced to death and his friends suggest that he flee Athens, he refuses on the grounds that he has no right to break the law—his "agreements and covenants" with the state. His adherence to the law is spiritual; violating "the most sacred laws" would be for the sake of "the miserable desire of a little more life."[2] Practicing justice overrides security and life itself. Socrates puts himself in the hands of the law, and by doing this he frees his spirit to pursue the truth about life and death; free of want, free to die, free to "depart in innocence, a sufferer and not a doer of evil; a victim, not of the laws but of men."[3] One can, however, easily identify with Socrates' disciples, who urge him to flee from death; they manifest the war between the psyche, which chooses life, and the soul, which has concerns that override even the natural will to survive.

McLean points out that growth in religious and spiritual health involves making conscious one's unconscious religion and spirituality. These are more important than one's manifest religion and spirituality. Neither a patient's religion nor his unconscious spirituality can be analyzed away "any

---

2. Plato, *Crito*, 437.
3. Ibid., 438.

more than his unconscious sexuality or anything else ever is."[4] (McLean notes that it is interesting for a patient to discover what is his or her unconscious religion. He or she may be Episcopalian but unconsciously Jewish or Buddhist.)

Unlike the psyche, which makes use of the false self for social purposes and attempts to comply with social norms, the soul rejects compliance, because compliance is falsity, which is anathema to the nature of the soul. In Judaism the essential deeds must be performed even when one is humiliated by others. The soul refuses to uncritically accept current opinion, and, living in perpetual wonder, insists on questioning cultural values. For example, Saint Teresa of Avila opens herself to a spiritual relation with God that puts worldly values in perspective. She begins to see the foolishness of being grieved by death's or by life's difficulties—not through an analysis of her grievances but through contacting truths of "sublime perfection." The poet Rainer Maria Rilke expressed the same sensibility:

> I have my dead, and I have let them go,
> and was amazed to see them so contented,
> so soon at home in being dead, so cheerful,
> so unlike their reputation.[5]

The spirit doesn't color what it sees; it sees clearly what is there and what the thing is worth in eternal time. The spirit enjoys an image for what it is. To idolize an image is to substitute it for the real thing, to call it the real thing, to act as if it is the real thing. The real thing delivers; the substitute gives a few minutes of satisfaction followed by a feeling of emptiness. Most of us are attracted to false images; we are drawn to movie stars because they project a luster that is temporarily pleasing. We are also easily gratified by falsity when it seems more attractive than the truth, often denying unpleasant facts about ourselves or about those to whom we are attached.

Culture provides fads and fashions. In the present culture a simple example is spending an inordinate amount of time and money on looking good, often exercising the body beyond its needs. The great religions may be affected by culture, but the resources of the great religions provide values and ideas that transcend culture. In the words of the Jewish author Bachya ben Joseph ibn Paquda, the believer "will always behold Him with his

---

4. McLean, "Health," 307.
5. Rilke, "Requiem," 73.

intellect and will continually revere Him, exalt Him, examine His works."[6] The believer lives in a relationship with God that is unlike the life lived by those who conform to the culture of their times: "He will see without physical eyes, hear without physical ears, speak without the tongue, sense things without their special organs; appraise them without reasoning."[7]

The need for attention to and representation of the spiritual part of life is expressed by the Christian monk Thomas Merton when he discusses one of the functions of the monk: the monk's most important service to the world is to be silent, to listen and to question, and to be exposed to "what the world ignores about itself—both good and evil."[8] Abandoning the world, mentally or physically or both, has positive uses for anybody whose commitment is to attend to deep neglected areas of reality. This is true for the artist, who needs solitude to tend to and replenish his or her soul in order to create, and for the person who is doing a spiritual account of his or her soul. "Solitude and seclusion from people save one from all the sins . . . and are the most powerful means for securing good qualities. The chief support for purity of heart is love of solitude and its acceptance."[9]

Abstention and renunciation have positive effects on the development of the soul. Abstention is a key to the spiritual life of Socrates. He obeys his "daemon," a kind of voice that only forbids but never commands him to do anything he is about to do. Socrates' way of life is a renunciation of accepted notions of security. He questions all beliefs. His spirit supersedes his desire to survive; it does not possess life nor is it possessed by life. Socrates achieves the ultimate renunciation: he dies for the idea of speaking his own mind in the face of threats from the rulers of Athens.

The psyche makes compromises. Unlike the psyche, the soul and the spirit do not compromise. That is not to say that the psyche has no integrity, just that its emphasis is elsewhere. Socrates' spirit says no to inclinations that may lead to a non-virtuous life. St. Teresa of Avila says no to the values of the world, sanctifying life by wanting nothing from it. She knows that within the convent there are subtle values at play that interfere with spiritual growth. She is aware that she has to struggle with her fondness of being liked by other people. She later achieves detachment: "As I am now out of the world, and my companions are few and saintly, I look down upon the

---

6. Bachya, *Duties*, 2:217.
7. Ibid.
8. Merton, *Contemplative Prayer*, 27.
9. Ibid.

world as from above and care very little what people say or what is known about me. I care more about the smallest degree of progress achieved by one single soul than for all the things that people may say about me."[10] Also, unlike the psyche, which sees its growth in accepting imperfections of oneself, the soul imagines perfect goodness and grieves whenever it falls short of it. Teresa experiences feelings of loneliness and abandonment when her soul suddenly remembers its absence from God.

The developed soul remains alive and unchanged in its integrity in the face of hardships. It has an unchangeable and immortal quality connected with its capacity to reflect then pass into solitude. A strong soul does not waver and may even feel joy in the face of harsh treatment, not because it is masochistic, but while aware of being insulted it is stirred by a vision of a good world where reparation is possible. The soul will often prefer its suffering if it means getting closer to God or to the truth. It sometimes sees suffering as unavoidable in a context of a search for truth.

Socrates and Saint Teresa exemplify a capacity to withstand grave difficulties, reflecting the indestructibility of God, goodness, and virtues. Dedicated to their vision, they spurn comforts, consolations, and the opinion of the world, creatively advancing in a fearless manner. Being subjected to attacks from opposing forces is part of their lives.

An example of a person with an unhealthy psyche and an uncompromising soul can be found in the philosopher Ludwig Wittgenstein. Wittgenstein, who was intolerant and dogmatic and close to being paranoid, was admired by those who encountered him for his "dedication to the discovery of truth at all costs,"[11] as Anthony Storr puts it.

Great spiritual and religious personalities, such as Dietrich Bonhoeffer, are in tune with the voice that calls them to lead a significant life. Bonhoeffer's response to the voice of his conscience, educated through the teachings of Christianity, was to return to Germany from the U.S. to fight the evil of the Nazis. In Germany he talked openly on the radio of the resistance movement, and he joined in a plot to kill Hitler. Had anyone said to Bonhoeffer that he was wasting his time and that what he was doing would not get the results he wanted, he would not have stopped. Bonhoeffer's alliance with and allegiance to the truth overrode personal and practical interests and brought him much suffering. In imitation of Jesus Christ he embodied a religious spirit that had emerged from and was based upon

---

10. Teresa, *Complete Works*, 298.
11. Storr, *Solitude*, 163.

his religious sensibility, training, and practice, and that guided him to lay down his life for others while feeling abandoned: "It belongs to the depth of the religious spirit to have felt forsaken, even by God."[12] Bonhoeffer felt the cost of losing his past, and the suffering, loneliness, and aloneness that accompany this experience; he prayed and heard a new thing:

> The past will come to you once more,
> and be your life's enduring part,
> through thanks and repentance.
> Feel in the past God's forgiveness and goodness,
> pray him to keep you today and tomorrow.[13]

Of course there are many secular heroic personalities who withstood great opposition, one of whom is Freud. In his *Interpretation of Dreams* Freud scrupulously takes account of his dreams and analyzes them for the purpose of understanding the human psyche, and this he does against all opposition.

The "dark night of the soul" in one's spiritual journey, which John of the Cross experiences, refers to loss of sense and understanding. The soul, in its dissatisfaction and suffering, finally abandons its own will and enters a state of faith and receptivity to the will of God. This experience has a value for the soul not unlike the value for the psyche, when one tolerates a depression "until it spontaneously lifts," and one "may come out of the depression stronger, wiser and more stable than before he or she went into it."[14]

Abandonment of one's will is close in sense and tone to abandonment of omnipotence, so important in a person's maturational process. This abandonment is usually met by great resistance because of the feeling of helplessness that follows. The psyche fears helplessness and sees it as an impediment to its advance, a form of unnecessary suffering, and it excludes experiences such as a healthy dependence on God or on any other enriching being and the existential dread of being exposed to that being. The soul endures fear of helplessness because it sees it as an existential fact, truth without illusion, and as an opening to get closer to God. The psyche is content with feeling secure when it masters itself and the environment. The very life of the soul entails continuous self-questioning, which, as Merton says, "brings us face to face with the ultimate meaning of our life." According to Merton, this self questioning "can never be without a certain

12. Bonhoeffer, *Letters*, 226.
13. Ibid.
14. Winnicott, "Depression," 77.

existential 'dread,'... a sense that one has somehow been untrue... to one's own inmost truth."[15]

Merton discusses the loss of soul in a description of the experience of mystical renewal, an "inner transformation brought about entirely by the power of God's merciful love, implying the 'death' of the self-centered and self-sufficient ego and the appearance of a new and liberated self who lives and acts 'in the Spirit.'"[16] If the old self seeks to imitate such transformation for its own advantage, the result is loss of soul:

> All falsity is disastrous in any relation with the ground of our own being and with God himself, who communicates with us through our own inner truth. To falsify our inner truth under pretext of entering into union with God would be a most tragic infidelity to ourselves first of all, to life, to reality itself and of course to God. Such fabrications end in the dislocation of one's entire moral and intellectual existence.[17]

Source materials of major religions, which provide examples and elucidation to help one transform one's character and change one's values, have been neglected because, in addition to having been misused, they have not been made relevant to modern life. There is a need to rescue notions such as virtue and sin from their misuse as tools for persecution and attribute to them their proper value. The value has been lost even among psychotherapists, who seem to embrace successfully a Buddhist psychological perspective as a methodology for decreasing suffering. More attention is paid to articles and books on meditation than, for example, to the first chapter of the Buddhist classic *The Path of Purification*. In this chapter the author talks about the need to abandon "covetousness" and "defilements." The chapter is replete with references to virtues such as wishing a person good, wishing him well, and wishing him joy; improper conduct such as wrong livelihood; and improper resort such as spending time with families who are "faithless, untrusting, abusive and rude, who wish harm, with ill, wish woe."[18] The rigor manifested in this chapter is the bedrock of Hinayana Buddhism; it is where the "stream enterer" begins. The tendency in the Western world, however, to substitute for these goals the achievement of "feel-good" and

---

15. Merton, *Contemplative Prayer*, 26.
16. Ibid., 110.
17. Ibid.
18. Buddaghosa, *Purification*, 18.

relaxed psychological states defeats the more rewarding, albeit exacting, Buddhist view.

Another source of strength is the writings of Moshe Chayim Luzzatto. He focuses on interior work and the values that impede it, as when he defines honor: "Honor is nothing but the vanity of vanities, which causes a man to defy his own mind and that of his Master and to forget his entire duty."[19]

Bachya entitled his book *Duties of the Heart*, stressing transformation of the inner life as paramount. Titles of chapters in the book, such as "Spiritual Accounting" and "Repentance," are preceded by the author's maxim in the first chapter: "In every act, public and private, the aim and purpose should be service of God for His name's sake, to please Him only, without thought of winning the favor of human creatures."[20] The notion of virtue in the life of the soul is vital. If one loses the concept of virtue one suffers the loss of emphasis and value accorded to character traits such as courage and truth. Similarly, one loses the force that the notion of sin lends to the act of murder or theft or betrayal. The soul examines itself for its own sake, not in order to advance the self or get along in the world, but in order to advance itself in virtue. Excessive ambition needs to be tempered, pride and vanity need to be diminished, and greed decreased; for example, in order for the soul to grow from within in a "right relationship" with God or with a principle of goodness outside herself. Any damage done by the soul is experienced as a self-inflicted wound that prevents the soul from achieving harmony, a harmony that manifests in fair-share relationships, in reconciliation between oneself and others and between the soul and God.

Psychoanalytical materials take into account one important religious concept, which in psychological terms is termed a capacity: the capacity to make reparation. The root of this capacity is an urge to repair damage done to oneself or others, a part of an individual's general drive to grow, psychologically, spiritually, biologically, and religiously. The healthy soul and the healthy psyche converge with regard to reparation and love. Religion is interested in transforming, neutralizing, or eradicating evil and in promoting good. The psychoanalyst Melanie Klein's concept of reparation concurs with the idea of transformation by emphasizing the possibility of making good one's bad impulses. Words such as *sacrifice* and *gratitude,* which appear in Klein's psychoanalytical theory, are unconscious references to the

---

19. Luzzatto, *Path*, 297.
20. Bachya, *Duties*, 2:11.

soul being alive in the act of reparation: "Side by side with the destructive impulses in the unconscious mind both of the child and of the adult, there exists a profound urge to make sacrifices, in order to help and to put right loved people who in fantasy have been harmed or destroyed."[21] Hence the psychotherapist makes reparation to the patient by facilitating the revival of his or her good impulses. The urge to repair, when identified with the psyche, is associated with guilt. When identified with the soul, the urge towards reparation is associated with repentance and regret—a natural ingredient in the life of an individual.

Problems of the soul can be distinguished from those of the psyche. Feeling anxiety about one's anger is a problem of the psyche. Holding on to the anger in spite of understanding its origins is a problem of the soul. Problems of the soul cannot be reduced to symptoms of psychological ill health, such as illusions or a persecuting conscience. A longing to be good could be motivated by love and not fear, and the desire for perfection is not necessarily a compulsive disorder. Acknowledgement of the damage one has done through hatred or envy is a sign of psychological progress, and confession of a habitual tendency to hate or envy can be the beginning of personal transformation.

The care of the soul, even in its most benign fashion, may be at the expense of the care of the psyche, and vice versa; this needs to be recognized and acknowledged. In pursuing one's highest values one may lose one's job or end a personal relationship. In transcending time a person detaches oneself from temporal time, which may have negative practical consequences. The person needs to know this to make a conscious, informed choice.

In the course of psychotherapeutic treatment of a person, something to think about is when, if, and under what circumstances the ailments of the psyche are symptomatic of a soul that will not take responsibility for its sins. Taking responsibility, confession, and repentance, in their healthy uses, are necessary for the growth of the soul. Along with making reparation they express the soul's creative response to the damage one produces.

A healthy prayer life benefits the psyche as well as the soul. Prayer enables a direct meeting with oneself—one's wishes and desires and sins, one's goodness and badness. The act of prayer indicates that a person wants to change; it is a way of breaking the vicious cycle, summoning the courage to resolve a conflict, or taking a stand when one is afraid.

---

21. Klein, "Love, Guilt," 311.

THOUGHTS ON PSYCHE, SOUL, AND SPIRIT

The spiritual approach to life is the ground for creative advance, yet the culture does not encourage spiritual growth. One can take permission and example for commitment and dedication to spiritual growth and spiritual values from the lives of saints and heroes. One learns from Socrates the value of examining one's life. One can ask, "Is this job worth doing? Is there non-monetary reward connected with this job? Do I love the job? Do I work with people whom I love? Will I have regrets about doing this job and about not going into another kind of work? Am I giving my enemy her fair share? Have I achieved one second of altruistic love today? What sins of omission have I committed in the last week towards my spouse? Have I implemented my interest in art lately? Did I betray my soul because I was afraid to confront my boss, or my friend?" One learns to act on the answers to these questions and take the consequences of one's choices.

If one's work does not fall into any category that the culture sanctions, or one is challenging the sanctioned corruption in an established institution, one will be attacked by those who envy the independence or by those who accept the corruption. If one loses confidence or loses one's job because of a moral or ethical stand one has taken, one can have mental companions such as Socrates. If one loses a friend because one no longer shares the same values, one can pray to St. Teresa for help in enduring the pain of separation. If the consequences of the stand one has taken are too hard to bear, one can find comfort in Bonhoeffer. Luzzatto will help when one feels trapped in the desire for honor. And Saint John of the Cross will accompany one through spiritual and creative aridity, when one feels distant from God and from everything one values.

9

ZOROASTRIAN PRAYERS AND THE CHARACTER OF AMERICA

ZOROASTRIANISM, THE IRANIAN RELIGION founded by Zarathustra some 3,000 years ago, is still practiced by about 200,000 people around the world, the highest concentration being in Iran and India. The most outstanding principle of Zoroastrianism is that evil is not simply the negation of good but a force that needs to be fought to the death. The creed cuts through grey shades in regard to evil and tips the scale in favor of determining clearly what is good and what is evil.

Zoroastrianism is a religion with life-size requirements. Unlike Christianity, which requires the formidable practice of turning the other cheek and loving all people, or Buddhism, which teaches the belief that goes against one's instincts—the belief that there is no abiding, unconditional self—Zoroastrianism focuses on what to an American are natural inclinations: "pursuit of happiness," and increase in goodness, honesty, freedom, enterprise, and intellect.

The Zoroastrian prayers in the sacred literature, the Avesta, consist of liturgical hymns and litanies. They include the Gathas, Zarathustra's hymns addressed to Ahura Mazda (Wise Lord), the supreme creator deity in Zoroastrianism, and litanies addressed to various deities or angels. The prayers contain a simple and straightforward emphasis on righteousness and truth, bases for the good life and for the war against evil. One prays to speak the truth, to be given the vision of truth, to be taught the truth of life, and to be true to oneself. Prayers for prosperity (the religion promotes individual and communal prosperity), so prevalent in the religion, satisfy a basic natural desire. Based on everyday commonsense—that is, instincts—the prayers reflect the simple and sober tenets of the Zoroastrian credo, which are a powerful antidote against an over-sophisticated, over-informed, and ironic American culture.

ZOROASTRIAN PRAYERS AND THE CHARACTER OF AMERICA

Many of the Zoroastrian prayers are holy formulas—spells that help one withstand evil, repel attacks of demons, and heal the sick. The most essential and the most powerful spell, the Ahunavar, is a recitation of the word spoken by Ahura Mazda before he created the universe. This prayer, a sacred formula of twenty-one words each of which represents a title of one of the twenty-one books of the Avesta, is a powerful weapon against the demons and the Evil Spirit itself, and as such is the essence of Ahura Mazda. The religion states that when recited with faith the Ahunavar inspires courage, and if all humanity recites it, it is potent enough to save the world from death. In essence the Ahunavar states that the most fundamental virtue is resignation to the will of Ahura Mazda, followed by righteousness, and that the blessings of the pure mind are given to those who serve the poor.

In his hymns of entreaty to Ahura Mazda, Zarathustra asks for revelation of the doctrine—best words and best deeds. One's task in the world is to align oneself with what is best and to cooperate with Ahura Mazda in the renovation of existence. Zoroastrianism embraces the material as well as the spiritual things of the world.

Though the religion has strong convictions about what is good and what is evil, and humanity's role and power in the renewal of existence, the Zoroastrian creed doesn't declare it the best religion, but a good one (thus warding off the pitfalls of religious chauvinism), and stresses choice and free will as viable and necessary. Each person must see and hear clearly what is good and what is bad and choose the good. One is also required, with the help of God's spirit (which the religion believes everyone possesses), to use independent judgment in regard to this choice. Phrases that appear in the Zoroastrian credo, like "through intuition we can learn," "May we reach You through our own Free-Will,"[1] and "if he asks this spirit (conscience) what he has to do, he will never go wrong,"[2] express a belief in a degree of autonomy. They are a strong reminder of America's original belief in and practice of self-reliance (with the help of God and other supernatural entities of course) and individualism.

The Zoroastrian hymns to deities and angels are addressed to the Sun, Moon, Waters, and Fire; to the angels that preside over these elements; and to the deity Mithra. These litanies have their origin in the polytheistic phase of Zoroastrianism and exemplify the Zoroastrians' desire to thrive. The Waters are praised for giving long life, increasing the stock of cattle,

1. Shavaksha, *Credo*, 49.
2. Ibid., 35.

and generally benefitting the village and the country of those who practice righteousness. The righteous ones are not only those who align themselves with what is good, but also those who use their power to intervene against spoilers of the good. A Zoroastrian, like his non-Zoroastrian American counterpart, whether an investment banker in New York or a farmer in the Midwest, is fully open by temperament and tradition to receiving unambiguously the rewards of his or her enterprise, self-exertion, and goodness. In Zoroastrianism the one who works hard will go to heaven as long as he or she is faithful to high standards of integrity. (In India, businesses have relied on the Parsi bankers for honest transactions.) Righteousness and discernment, true speech, and good words and deeds temper and mitigate what would otherwise be an American gospel of greed.

In Zoroastrianism goodness and truth, which comprise righteousness, shade into one another; good thoughts shades into true thoughts, good words into truth, and good deeds into just deeds. The prayers seem to issue from a conflict-free true self, one that is clear of artifice and sophistry, reviving and exhilarating one's own true self. In the morning prayer of the Litany to the Sun one asks to further a good thought, a more straightforward thought. In that prayer the health of the body is connected with righteousness; one asks for goodness for the soul and for the body. At midday there is a prayer for the soul to attain a light higher than the high (nothing short of the highest). And in the evening the prayer to the "Bountiful Spirit," the sun, is for a change from evil to good, affirming that through Ahura Mazda good will triumph over evil. The Litany to the Sun includes praise of good thoughts, good words, and good deeds, of the present and the future, and the renunciation of evil thoughts, evil words, and evil deeds. Praising these entities of goodness themselves grants them autonomy and a powerful existence.

The Litany to the Moon includes a pledge to sacrifice to it for gathering strength to withstand the attacks of evil. The Moon is a nourishing entity, radiant and glorious, possessing warmth, knowledge, goodness, and the power to heal. Mithra, and the litany to him, seem to reflect what is to some extent incumbent upon the Zoroastrian practitioner. Mithra, protector of truth and guardian of cattle, the harvest, and waters, is true and exalted and helpful, but mainly he is "ever wakeful," with a thousand ears and ten thousand eyes. He is praised for being everywhere, "in the country" and "above the country."[3] And though no person is capable of being "ever

---

3. Dhalla, *Nyaishes*, 71.

ZOROASTRIAN PRAYERS AND THE CHARACTER OF AMERICA

wakeful," the Zoroastrian, by virtue of his or her keen attention to his or her words, thoughts, and deeds, is bound to be as alert and watchful over himself or herself as one could ever hope to be.

Pragmatic issues in Zoroastrianism seem to fit the American imagination and goals. Think, for instance, of life in abundance, a skillful tongue, extensive memory, and an excellent intellect, which one asks to be delivered by the element of Fire, one of the most important sacred symbols in Zoroastrianism, which purifies wrongdoers in the next lifetime and protects them in this one. Or wisdom in the timeliness of an action, the ability to assess in advance the gain and the loss of an action, the ability to complete an action, and farsightedness—"knowing much from little." The Litany to Fire requests prompt action in well-being and nourishment. And what would crown this better but a belief in a God, Ahura Mazda, who is none other than a "Bounteous Spirit"?

The litanies call upon the angels who preside over the bounteous Sun, the meritorious Moon, the onward-moving Waters, and heroic Fire, including the ever-wakeful Mithra, the all-seeing one. They ask for acts of increase and furtherance and advancement in good thoughts, purity of body, and righteousness in the world, painting a picture of a civilization that is enthusiastic and hopeful, the way America had been in its inception and still is in its innermost heart.

The litanies don't flinch from asking for strength and victory and for a swift victory over evil—vanquishing adversaries and enemies at one stroke. The enemy, described in the Litany to the Sun, consists of thieves and tyrants, sorcerers and fairies, so different from a subtler enemy, such as a Buddhist demon who distracts the devotee from meditating, an obstacle in one's mind. Zoroastrian thieves can be thought of as subtler obstacles as well—thieves who lurk in oneself, who rob the soul of its natural resources, and the sorcerers can be imagined as cultural sorcerers who silence one's true self with the worship of fame and the media.

In the Zoroastrian prayers one senses a freedom to ask for more, no inhibition about asking for better, and though some of the prayers refer to simple early agricultural life, there is a sense of the philosopher Whitehead's notions of creative advance and the aim of life, which is to live, to live well, and to live better. The religion weaves the spiritual and material aspects of existence: the Moon is wise and also a giver of fortune. The early Zoroastrian asks for "fully developed men" but also for more cattle. Angels who personify abundance are asked to manifest themselves, along with their great glory and joy, but meals and bread are also requested and are earned by self-exertion. And as we continue to pray we can't help but be moved, spiritually and physically, by the audacity that the words of the prayers emit—words such as progress, affluence, healing, courage, joy, vigor, and victory, bursting with a healthy unabated energy. They are healthy because nowhere is there a sense of compulsion or rigidity, or of stalemate. The tone is of optimism and hope; the future is full of promise.

The Zoroastrian opposition to extremes such as asceticism reflects the religion's unstrained relationship with the divine. Zarathustra's approach to Ahura Mazda is fervent yet levelheaded. His outstretched hands seem unshaken, and his poet's voice, though questioning, is unfaltering. His is a democratic approach—he is not afraid to cut across hierarchic barriers. Though Zarathustra perceives Ahura Mazda as awesome, "all-knowing" and "all-seeing," he seeks his God as a friend and equal: "This I ask thee, O Lord, answer me truly: May a wise one like thee reveal it to a friend such as I am. . . . And as Righteousness may he lend us his friendly support."[4] The Lord's friendly support indicates his forbearance and constancy rather than omniscience and omnipotence. Ahura Mazda shares in one's distress, and friendship with him is promised as a reward to those who please Zarathustra.

Zarathustra's hymns and most of the other liturgical hymns are in the first person. In these hymns, the petitioner who praises, sacrifices to, venerates, and repents before Ahura Mazda and the angels has a personal relationship with them. There is a sense that when the petitioner asks for power and renewal and joy Ahura Mazda listens and will grant these requests. The two are close. In addition to God as a friend to humankind, fire is a friend also, and humankind is a sworn friend to righteousness. God and humanity collaborate in renovating existence, overcoming evil and, as one of the hymns states, promoting the house, street, city, village, and country.

---

4. Duchesne-Guillemin, *Hymns*, 65.

10

THE ISRAELI/PALESTINIAN CONFLICT: A NEW BEGINNING[1]

> *This essay differs from the other essays in this book in its subject matter. It is an essay that involves politics, and it aims towards a pragmatic solution to a conflict that has ravaged two nations, the Israeli and the Palestinian. We included the essay to bring forth religious, spiritual, and philosophical notions that may add to and help a process towards peace.*

THE MANY PROBLEMS BETWEEN the Israelis and the Palestinians, the wars that have ensued and the failed negotiations that followed, are rooted in the events of the Zionist immigration that took place at the turn of the twentieth century. Taking into account the many factors that continually exacerbate the Israeli/Palestinian conflict, this essay sheds new light on possible ways out of the impasse, using fresh ideas from luminary thinkers and passages in Jewish and Islamic scriptures as sources of creative advance towards a new beginning. From the turn of the twentieth century and for decades afterward the Jews bought land from Arabs in Palestine, disenfranchising the fellahin of their land. The Zionists paid for every plot of land. Nevertheless it was an act of robbery, metaphorically speaking. The Arab leaders, the large landowners among the notable effendi, with the Ottomans and the British as enablers, were silently complicit in the land deals, treating the fellahin as if they did not deserve being accounted for. Though there were several groups involved, and though, according to the historian K. W. Stein, these social and economic changes would have been delayed but not halted even if the Jews had not acquired the land, the damage inflicted by the Jews became a cause célèbre. Palestinians' early frustration and rage about their plight broke out in riots, massacres, and a revolt in the 1920s and 30s. It intensified after the victories of Israel in the wars of 1948 and 1967, which

---

1. Originally published online in *Tikkun*, May 1, 2009. http://www.tikkun.org/article.php/BerghashJillson.

resulted in the annexation of more land, and has erupted in increasing violence, including intifadas, suicide bombings, and launching of rockets into Israel from 1987 to the present day.

Interestingly robbery, considered immoral when related to humankind, is, according to the philosopher A. N. Whitehead, inextricably tied with life. He reminds us that life is robbery, and that all living societies, from the lowest forms to human beings, proceed by robbery. For the Jews the purchase of land in Palestine was a healthy robbery (a paradoxical notion), in that it was life giving and life enhancing, providing a place to survive—a moral imperative—and a future, an opportunity to build a better life than the life they led in Europe. In the nineteenth and twentieth centuries, as the philosopher T. Kapitan notes, virulent anti-Semitism was a fact of life for European Jews, manifested in persecutions and pogroms. The survival of the Jewish people as Jews required a place of refuge where they could manage affairs in their own way without being constantly under vicious attacks and living with the perpetual stigma of minority status—in short, a nation. Thus, the Zionists urged the Jews to leave their countries of birth and settle in Palestine. The problem would become more acute after the Holocaust in World War II. The poet Dan Pagis, a Holocaust survivor, writes about it:

> Imaginary man, go. Here is your passport.
> You are not allowed to remember . . .
> Don't escape with the sparks
> inside the smokestack . . . You've got a decent coat now,
> a repaired body, a new name
> ready in your throat.
> Go, You are not allowed to forget.[2]

While the robbery was healthy for the Jews, it was unhealthy for the Palestinians. It lacked moral responsibility, which requires concern about the general good beyond self-interest. The Palestinians were now exposed to modern secularism and to new agricultural methods, which they felt as an affront. They experienced transformation of their customs; informal dealings were replaced by a formal bureaucracy, and a barter economy gave way to a market economy. They lost the prestige of the past and their way of life, a change too great for some of them to handle. They lost land their ancestors had inhabited for generations. Villages disappeared. The 1948 war brought the conflict to a head. Many villages were destroyed and

---

2. Pagis, "Instructions," 130.

many Palestinians went into exile. Would the Jews have been able to create a homeland had they worked to prevent losses to the Arabs? Whitehead points out that the robber requires justification: is the robber making a positive creative use of what was stolen? Does the robbery increase his chances for survival?

When the Zionists came to Palestine in great numbers after World War I they succeeded in purchasing land and moving into it without real opposition, due in part to the dire agrarian circumstances of the Palestinians. Other factors aided purchase of land by the Zionists. In the first place, the Ottoman Empire had unequivocally helped the Arab notable effendi to purchase and possess land at the expense of Arab peasants, placing them in a position of total control over selling it. Secondly, the peasants were not experienced in confronting the bureaucratic and legislative machinery of the Ottomans or the British. They were simple and uneducated, lacking verbal and writing skills, whereas most Zionists were accustomed to using verbal and written negotiations with various hostile regimes while in exile. The peasants were not able to stand up to the greed of the effendi classes and the need of the Zionists. The British, who ruled Palestine from 1918 to 1947 under the Mandate, acted as a mediator but did nothing to help the condition of the fellahin.

The Palestinian peasants and the Arab political leadership itself were fractured by ties of kinship and family, and by local rivalries, village identity, and personal connections, all due to clan self-interest. Thus, they were not able to form a united front to protect themselves from being exploited. To the degree that they were united, it was on the basis of what they were against, not what they were for—repeatedly expressing their rage over the Jewish presence in sporadic acts of violence. There were also contradictions in the mentality of the Palestinian leadership: on the one hand they made anti-Zionist statements, on the other hand they were involved in land sales.

The lack of unity among Palestinians continues. The philosopher and university president S. Nusseibeh describes the structure of Fatah in the 1980s as having a "militant arm" and a "diplomatic" one, which apparently did not always work in agreement. And, with the spread of Islamic education in the West Bank and Gaza, ideological competition between the PLO and Islamists resulted in verbal quarrels, which turned into fistfights. In 2007 the rivalry of Fatah and Hamas escalated into killing. In general, instead of "cleaning house" the Palestinians, to deflect responsibility for general infighting and violence among their factions, have allowed themselves to be seduced by the fallacy of post hoc reasoning: they claim that their infighting, including family squabbles and even murders of kin and neighbor, is entirely due to the Israeli occupation. Nusseibeh, although emphasizing that the main problem for the Palestinians is the Israeli occupation, notes, "The PA's weakness can be traced back to all the familiar homegrown problems of corruption, bad management, and so on."[3] For years the leadership of the PA pocketed money that had been intended for the general population.

Throughout history, the Jews have shown an extraordinary will to preserve life; this characteristic appears in Jewish scriptures, where the preservation of life is a high and strong value and a priority in several commandments. As Rolland's character Jean Christophe says, "The Bible is the bone and sinew of nations with the will to live." The prophet Jeremiah is known for his prophecy of doom, but what is less discussed is his emphasis on life. He exhorted the Israelites to compromise and accept exile instead of death at the hands of the Babylonians, foreseeing that the exile would have positive results in the future and that the Israelites and their heritage would survive. Most probably, were he living today Jeremiah would further the urge to live at the expense of possessing occupied land. Visionary and pragmatic, he responded to the circumstances of his time as they were unfolding. As he prophesied, the Israelites did return to their land. Nowadays the compromises necessary for survival would of course take forms different from exile, such as withdrawal of settlements.

Thousands of years after Jeremiah, again life's urge was a catalyst for the Jews, this time propelling the Zionists towards the realization of their vision of building a homeland. They did it in an astonishing novel fashion. Their path was parallel to the way of the universe, in which evolution takes place in intense creative experience. The Jews' talent for enterprise, issuing in creative advance, is evident in Israel today, where the economy, stirred by imagination, is booming, in large part due to an innovative technological industry that attracts large companies from all over the world.

Most Jews, cherishing the opportunity to build a homeland that would help them survive, were insensitive to the loss to the Palestinians; they saw the Palestinians as less than life-size, diminishing the significance of their worth as individuals and as a community. Thus, the dilemma of the Jews' indisputable need for a homeland, on the one hand, and the usurpation of Arab land, the tragic loss to the Palestinians, on the other hand, remains

---

3. Nusseibeh, *Palestinian Life*, 421.

THE ISRAELI/PALESTINIAN CONFLICT

unresolved. But the onus for resolving the ongoing conflict, then as now, is not just on Israel. Palestinians need to acknowledge their passivity and the corruption of their leaders, and the suffering these leaders have caused and continue to cause the Israelis and their own people by condoning if not instigating actions of extreme violence.

There have always been Jews concerned about the plight of the Palestinians—from Brit-Shalom, a small Jewish group, which was founded in 1925, to B'tzelem, a current Israeli human rights group. But throughout the years the voice of these groups has been, for the most part, drowned out by the fervent avowals of the more nationalistic Jews, whose interest has been to preserve the nation without consideration for the other side. The theologian Reinhold Niebuhr emphasizes that the conduct of a nation, which is based on its self-interest, always takes precedence over moral considerations. Acting like a typical nation, the Zionists were strengthened by their devotion to their mission of building a homeland for the Jews. Their perseverance was expressed through great sacrifice of self-interest: profit, convenience, comfort, and family life—in sum, any kind of personal advantage. Their commitment increasingly endowed them with power and freed them to exercise a strong national will, to the point where their aspirations, which culminated in patriotism, transmuted into "national egoism." As Niebuhr says, the unqualified character of a zealous devotion is "the very basis of the nation's power and of the freedom to use the power without moral restraint. Thus the unselfishness of individuals makes for the selfishness of nations."[4]

As individuals, some Israelis and some Palestinians believe in giving fair share to the other side. Put into a group, however, most of them act unjustly; selfish reasons predominate and justice is compromised. Niebuhr continues to say that a nation cannot be critical of itself without endangering the very base on which it is founded—its unity. It cannot acknowledge its evil without destroying the fervent devotion of its members, on which it relies for survival. The loyalty of Zionists was of such high intensity that a critical approach (generally typical of Jews) towards the usurpation of Arab land was relinquished.

But there is something more at stake than unity within each nation. The context for both nations has changed since Israel's beginnings, which seems to show that without self-criticism destruction is inevitable. Israel is no longer dealing with a submissive Palestinian population. The method of

---

4. Niebuhr, *Moral Man*, 91.

appropriating Palestinian land no longer serves the purpose of securing a Jewish homeland. The "new Zionists" who are building the settlements are robbing land neither for the survival of the Jews nor for their security, but to realize their ideological claim to the land. In addition, this robbery causes undue misery to the Palestinians. As for the Palestinian extremists, their method of violence boomerangs—their quality of life deteriorates severely. Obsessed with taking over the land and with punishing Israel with violent acts, which aims at preventing Israelis from living normal lives, they lose track of what is in their basic self-interest—survival. Thus, self-criticism of present methods and acknowledgment of past missteps are essential if resulting divisions are to be contained and consensus is to be achieved without violence. Niebuhr's point concerning the self-interest of nations needs to be qualified to include circumstances in which a nation, to strengthen its self-interest, will tolerate temporary divisions, learn from its mistakes, and move forward.

The Zionists had been able to fulfill what Whitehead says is the function of reason—promoting the art of life and directing an attack on the environment, adapting it to their interests. The word *attack* in this context is used by Whitehead in a positive way, indicating an urge to live, to live well, to live better. The Zionist attack on the environment ranged from persuading the British government to do what they wanted to establishing a nucleus for homeland, buying barren land from Arab landowners, and transforming it into fertile land.

One of the great assets of the Zionists was that they combined a vision, ideals, and intention with efficient methods of realizing their ideals. Theodore Herzl was the visionary, the first to speculate on the possibility of a homeland for the Jews. His vision had a creative power that effected its realization only in an environment that would satisfy Jewish longing (Uganda would not do). Chaim Weizmann was the expeditor who used practical reason to seek, as Whitehead puts it, "an immediate method of action," a kind of reason "that is shared with the foxes."[5] Not only were the Zionists able to adapt to the authorities and to the harsh reality of Eretz-Yisrael, but also they were able to change the thinking of the authorities in their favor and to transform the land for their benefit. In 1918 Weizmann was able, for instance, to influence the British to oppose loans for the fellahin. His skills of persuasion reflect thinking that goes back as far as the second century BC, when a Chinese philosopher who was distinguished by his pragmatic approach pointed out that, "On the whole, the difficult

---

5. Whitehead, *Reason*, 10, 11.

thing about persuasion is to know the mind of the person one is trying to persuade and to be able to fit one's words to it."[6] Weizmann persistently pressed on to achieve his goal, which may be characterized in Whitehead's words as a victory of persuasion over force—a mark of civilization. It is likely that through the power of persuasion the Jews succeeded in gaining access to the formulation of ordinances and agreements developed by the British that were designed to halt their land purchase from the Arabs. This discovery resulted in finding other ways to purchase land.

By building a nucleus for the state the Zionists freed themselves from repeating the past, entering upon a new and fresh adventure, a "novel contrast" to the Jewish exilic life, whereas the Palestinians froze the past, clinging to their ways, perpetuating intracommunal strife and submitting uncritically to their leaders. The primary experience of the Arab peasants was surviving against nature. They never adapted to the Ottoman rule or the British Mandate, much less to the environment itself, that is, transforming the environment for their own purposes. They obstructed creativity, life, by their passivity.

In addition, the Palestinian peasantry lacked a vision for a better future, foresight, and a clear political goal. As a result they did not have a policy that could lead them to take charge of their future and build a national home. The First National Covenant met in Jerusalem as late as 1964. The lack of vision or purpose on the part of Palestinians is evident today. Mahdi Abdul Hadi, director of the Palestinian research institute Passia, was quoted as saying, "In Palestinians history there are no goals—no beginnings, nor ends. There are unfolding chapters, like waves in the sea. The Aksa [the militant off-shoot of Al-Fatah] are swimming with the tide, but they don't know where it will take them."[7] Discussing the neglect of the Old City of Jerusalem, inhabited by Palestinians who suffered under Israel's rule after the 1967 war, Nusseibeh notes, "Palestinian leaders barely did a thing to defend their rights in the Old City or to promote its development. By boycotting municipal elections, they willfully relinquished the most potent democratic weapon available to them for pushing economic and social development."[8] He also notes that when he took the post of president of Al-Quds University in Jerusalem, it was "a microcosm of the many ills besetting Palestinian society. It was poor,

---

6. Han Fei Tzu, *Basic Writings*, 73.
7. Kershner, "Fatah Militants."
8. Nusseibeh, *Palestinian Life*, 168.

shoddily run, and seething with religious fanaticism."[9] A recent three-year plan, "Building a Palestinian State," gives voice to Palestinians who in addition to criticizing the Israeli occupation take responsibility for their insufficient attention to shortcomings in the areas of governance, law and order, and basic service delivery.

The Palestinians' loss—any loss—reflects the hard truth that at the core of life there is loss, and that loss is evil. That this is true is an offense to our sensibilities. After all, life is creative; evil is destructive. Nevertheless, paradoxically, life proceeds through inevitable loss—selection and elimination of obstacles—to establish a new order of things. In an unpublished interview with Rachel Berghash, Robert Hass quoted a Cathar sermon from the thirteenth century that goes so far as to say, "If the world were not evil in itself every choice would not constitute a loss." The Bible has examples of selection—fathers selecting one sibling at the expense of the other. It is ironic that to evade the evil of obstruction and to proceed with life we must commit the evil act of selecting. The patriarchs Abraham and Isaac are persuaded by their wives to follow the divine plan of selection. Isaac is chosen over Ishmael and Jacob is chosen over Esau. Isaac is selected to be a patriarch of an emerging great nation. Amends to Hagar and Ishmael—the promise to make Ishmael into a nation—though substantial, seem like recompense, minor when compared to the promise held for Isaac and his descendants. The selection of Isaac and the exclusion of Ishmael is an act necessary for the birth of Judaism. This act, in its very evil, is life.

Jacob, as promised by God, is selected to carry on the legacy of Abraham and to secure the growth of the Jews into a nation. The legacy of blessings and prosperity will bear fruit only by excluding Esau, an obstruction to the goal. Jacob's life as an inheritor of his father's legacy proceeds by robbing Esau of his birthright (although Esau sold it to him). That the selection, deception, and exclusion was followed by the birth of the Jewish nation justifies the robbery.

Some prophets and most Jewish commentators on the Bible consider Esau an evil man. His anguish over his loss does not evoke their sympathy. A few examples in the Torah make up for the lack of wider sympathies (notwithstanding Isaac's sympathy) in the original Esau story, reflecting the fact that alternative feelings had simmered in the background and were given expression later on. Moses commands the Israelites, "Do not hate an

---

9. Ibid., 386.

Edomite [a descendent of Esau] for he is your brother."[10] Preceding this is the command in which the Israelites are required to take heed and not to violate the territory of Esau's children: "You are about to pass through the territory of your brothers the descendants of Esau, who live in Seir. They will be afraid of you, but be very careful. Do not provoke them to war, for I will not give you any of their land, not even enough to put your foot on. I have given Esau the hill country of Seir as his own."[11] A later example is in the Midrash: Rabbi Shmelke from Nikolsburg is one of the few who is sensitive to Esau's suffering. A Hasid master, he was moved by the tears of Esau, and he referred to the Midrash that says that the Messiah will not come before the tears of Esau have ceased to flow, and he added that the tears of Esau "are the tears which all human beings weep when they ask something for themselves, and pray for it."[12] The sensitivity to Esau and his descendents in some in the Torah and the Midrash redeems the evil committed against Esau, making the evil of his loss tragic rather than gross and unmitigated.

It is in the power of religious leaders of both nations to deal with the loss suffered by their people. It is in the realm of their duties to acknowledge that loss is evil, a reality to deal with—not promote—requiring a broadening of sympathy. These leaders need to encourage compromise, which, although it involves loss, avoids the destruction brought about by intransigent positions. The Qur'an proposes a methodology to transcend feelings of loss: "Through the passage of time, verily human beings are in a state of loss, except those who have faith, and do righteous deeds, and join together in the mutual enjoining of truth, and of patient perseverance."[13] The religious leaders need to recognize the metaphysical truth that loss is inherent in existence beyond the reach of temporal solutions, since ultimately, at the deepest level, as Whitehead notes, evil is about the fact that the past fades; yet everything is saved and purified in God.

Religious extremists among Israelis and Palestinians, in order to fortify their existing views, in which they have made enormous investments of time, money, and passion, use various forms of fallacious reasoning. For example, they appeal to the authority of tradition and the authority of God, which hinders pragmatic solutions to the conflict. Their appeal to

10. Deut 23:7. All biblical quotations in this essay are from the Jerusalem Bible.
11. Deut 2:4–5.
12. Buber, *Tales*, 1:186.
13. Sultan, *Qur'an* 103, 69.

the authority of God doesn't leave much room for human decision among those who believe in it. As the philosopher of pragmatism C. S. Peirce puts it so vividly, the method of authority fixes belief by teaching and reiterating certain doctrines to the young, by terrifying into silence or even massacring those who reject the beliefs of the establishment. This phenomenon is prevalent among Muslims nowadays who attempt, often violently and through threats, to force the "infidels," among their own people and others, to believe in the doctrine they believe in. There is a passage in the Qur'an, however, that opposes this practice: "Let there be no compulsion in religion. Truth stands out clear from falsehood. Whoever rejects evil and believes in God has grasped the most trustworthy handhold that never breaks."[14]

On both sides the extremists' appeal to the authority of God assumes that God is solely on one side—one's own. The cause of their fanaticism is identifying the lust of their hearts, their personal inclinations, with the voice of God. The religious leaders of these extremists are absorbed by their love for their people and what they consider their land. To defend their views they use a priori reasoning based on their tradition and divine authority. But this love for their people, this goodness, although seemingly moral—to assure their own survival—shades into egotism, narrow and unfeeling towards the other. It reduces God to a personal commodity, a servant of the ego, a God of narrow sympathies—no longer the God of all-benevolence towards one group or another—to the point of being very like evil. This egotism diminishes God to a finite being, a God of settling for less than what can be, thus ignoring the infinite freedom and the infinite possibilities that are in the nature of God.

A God serving the interests of only one group, defending land for only one group, and seeming to pit one group against another is a warrior God, an uncompromising avenger: "The God with whom you have made terms may be the God of destruction, the God who leaves in his wake the loss of the greater reality."[15] Thus religious leaders, instead of meddling in issues such as land and power, are called upon to inspire new feelings—tender feelings amongst peoples that belong to the goodness of God and his creation. The idea of the goodness of God and God's creation appears in both Judaism and Islam. In Judaism, "The Lord is good to all: and his tender mercies are over all his works."[16] As to the goodness of God, "And

---

14. Sultan, *Qur'an* 2:256, 149.
15. Whitehead, *Religion*, 17.
16. Ps 145:9 (JB).

God saw everything that he has made, and behold, it was very good."[17] This good original creation is dynamic; God proceeds to renew it daily: "and in His goodness renews daily, perpetually, the work of creation."[18] In Islam, Al-Barr, the source of all goodness, is the seventy-ninth name of God in the Qur'an. The dynamic nature of the goodness of creation appears in the writing of the Sufi sage Ibn Arabi, who says that creation is renewed at every instant.

Another contentious issue that stems from religious belief in the authority of God is the concept of the Holy Land and the Holy City. Designating a place as holy and having many people concur is sufficient for considering a place as such. The poet Abba Kovner, while illuminating the significance of bestowing a value on the physical world, illustrates this point:

> Mount Zion does it really exist or
> is it like our love that glows from another light/rising night
> after night?[19]

But the concept of a holy place has created an acute problem between extremist Jews and Muslims, distracting from the need to share the land in an equitable fashion. A holy place, a meaningful concept in itself, has become like the golden calf—meaningless, empty, used to compensate for the lack of something of worth. The Holy Land has become an object of idolatry, masking a feeling of acquisition, used to justify acts of violence. The extremists do not take into account that the attribution of holiness to where God dwells is not about possessing the land and fighting for it, but about a holy life brought about by God's presence in the land. It is the holiness of God and the holiness of life that must not be violated. Thus, viewing the land as an end and worshipping it robs the ultimate object of worship, God, of inherent value.

A Sufi story beautifully illustrates the idea of a place designated as holy in the service of a holy life: a Sufi told of how the first time he made the pilgrimage he saw the Ka'ba but not the lord of the Ka'ba; the second time he saw both the Ka'ba and the lord of the Ka'ba. The third time he saw the lord of the Ka'ba but not the Ka'ba.

---

17. Gen 1:31.
18. Scherman, *ArtScroll*, 93.
19. Kovner, "I don't know," 117.

PSYCHE, SOUL, AND SPIRIT

Peirce proposes the pragmatic method as an antidote to rigid thinking, the uncritical submission to authoritarian doctrine. His method incorporates the necessity of considering the practical bearing of our ideas, on the basis of results from past experience, and entertaining all the conceivable events that are probable or might occur if one's ideas are applied. For instance, all decisions that involve both the Palestinian and the Israeli sides need to be bilateral, not unilateral, as has been the case in the conflict. As early as 1939 philosopher A. N. Whitehead foresaw tragic consequences to making unilateral decisions: "In the adjustment of Jews and Arabs, one-sided bargains are to be dreaded. They spell disaster for the future."[20] These proceedings are necessary to avoid surprise ("O, another intifada!"). Since 1967 Israeli governments, on both the left and the right, have given only lip service to the policy of ceasing to build settlements and expand existing ones. They have failed to conceive of the rage and helplessness and violent responses that these "facts on the ground" evoke among Palestinians, and the anguish and the trauma it will cause the settlers, if the two-state solution were implemented and some settlements dismantled. The matter of the wall that Israel has erected is pragmatic in terms of Israel's present security—it has stopped suicide bombing in Israel. But because the wall has bisected villages, separating Palestinian farmers from their vineyards, it has increased suffering and hatred toward Israel among Palestinians and the likelihood of violence in the future.

Another failure to conceive of results is Hamas' takeover of Gaza, which has been a blow to Fatah, Israel, and the U.S. The victory of Hamas in the 2006 general election was a surprise to the world; Hamas was not given proportionate power, and the world did not foresee that this would result in their rage and their violent takeover of Gaza. On the other hand, forty years earlier, in 1967, Levi Eshkol, the prime minister of Israel, notwithstanding his cautiousness and his fear of U.S. disapproval in regard to Israel's plan to start a war on the Arabs, was concerned, to his credit, about the conceivable results of that decision. He questioned the plan, to the chagrin of his army generals and the majority of the Israeli population: "If we conquer, what then?"

When a nation aims for dominance the result is the decline of that nation. Whitehead describes what happens when the dominance of a system, a principle, a way of thinking takes precedence:

> The history of the Mediterranean lands and of Western Europe is the history of the blessing and the curse, of political organizations,

---

20. Kapitan, *Perspectives*, 36.

of religious organizations, of schemes of thought, of social agencies for large purposes. The moment of dominance, prayed for, worked for, sacrificed for, by generations of the noblest spirits, marks a turning point where the blessing passes into the curse. Some new principle of refreshment is required.[21]

The fear and distrust between Israel and Palestine is by now so encompassing, so habitual, that to dominate and terrorize the other seems like the only solution. But the one dominated constitutes an underlying ongoing threat to the dominating power, which is also weakened by a tendency to complacency. A plea that deflects the notion of dominance appears in the Qur'an: "Say: 'O People of the Book, come to common terms as between us and you: that we worship none but God; that we erect not, from among ourselves, lords and patrons other than God.'"[22] Nusseibeh tells a tale about the time Caliph Omar journeyed to the Holy City "and a Jew helped Omar to locate the place of the Rock over which the temple once stood."[23] Having found it, he cleaned the rock with his own robe as a token of service, in that way shying away from declaring himself the master of it. Emphasis on creative resources in the respective religions and cultures, such as the ones quoted above, can be an antidote to violence and dominance, to seeing each other as an unredeemed enemy, thus engendering mutual trust.

Both Israelis and Palestinians have been dominated by the idea that if they don't retaliate the other side will think they're weak and come back in greater force. In general, the practice of violent retaliation begets only violent retaliation. It does not work; it does not resolve a conflict in ways that promote life. The momentary satisfaction of retaliating obscures the fact that each side justifies its own acts of retaliation, refusing to apply the justification to the other side. Many religious leaders among the extremists in both nations are especially culpable of this self-righteous position; it is the other who is evil, who only understands force and is in need of redemption. They do not acknowledge that the evil in the enemy is also in themselves. These leaders, using political propaganda in the guise of divine authority and tradition, inflame their followers, who then act in ways that are violent, adding to loss of life.

Cooperation is the productive, pragmatic alternative to dominance. Evolution through cooperation is one of the ways of the universe. Of the

---

21. Whitehead, *Process*, 399.
22. Sultan, *Qur'an*, 3:64, 151.
23. Nusseibeh, *Palestinian Life*, 532.

requirement regarding modesty, Abravanel, a fifteenth-century Jewish philosopher and interpreter of scripture, said it is "the inwardness of true piety hidden from the world at large."[24] The Qur'an stresses moral character as the quintessential religious feature: "The Prophet was asked, 'Which Muslim has the perfect faith?' He answered, 'One who possesses the best moral character.'"[25] (The "business" of religion is not, as some religious leaders would have it, to focus on immediate appearance, such as mere repetition of prayers, sexual mores, and modest attire, which indicate a decay of religion.) In the pursuit of commonality, it would be pragmatic for the religious leaders of Judaism and Islam to convene and constitute a kind of spiritual collective mind.

A new idea to counter dominance and remedy injustice was conceived by Gandhi: nonviolent resistance. It worked. Gandhi did not even consider undesirable alternatives such as retaliation to violence. He, and Martin Luther King Jr., who followed his ideas, adopted the path of not undesirable alternatives, such as civil disobedience. The distinction between a desirable and a not undesirable alternative is an important one. If there were an increase in the number of inspired leaders and ordinary people in Palestine who used civil disobedience to protest the violence of Israel and the violence of their own people, they could affect the policy of the government. When Israel built the wall that bisected the soccer field in Al Quds University, Nusseibeh, its president, and his colleagues successfully ran a nonviolent protest that aimed at conquering the Israelis with ideas and persuasions. However, Nusseibeh's few successful attempts at nonviolent resistance did not take hold and spread. According to him, his attempts were rejected by some Palestinians (he was beaten by his students) and by the government of Israel, who put him in prison on some pretext.

It is incumbent upon religious leaders to interpret law and tradition with a freshness that is in contrast to the system dominated by old ideas that have become fodder for hatred and suspicion—ideas such as Israel's biblical right to the land, and Palestinians' right to the land because of having lived there for centuries. These old ideas risk life being embalmed alive. A remarkable example of the contrast between system and freshness used for creative advance is seen in the steps taken by Yochanan ben Zakai, the Jewish sage who lived after the destruction of Jerusalem in 70 AD. During the siege of the city by the Romans he was not allowed to leave the city but

24. Abravanel, *Etz Hayim*, 917.
25. Sultan, *Qur'an*, 119.

was able to sneak out in a coffin carried by his students. He then negotiated with Vespasian, a Roman general, to spare the town of Yavneh along with its scholars. According to Talmudic tradition he predicted that the general would become emperor. When this happened Vespasian met Yochanan ben Zakai's requests and granted him permission to re-establish the Sanhedrin and to found a new center of Jewish law and study in Yavneh.

Yochanan ben Zakai led the council of Yavneh, from which emerged rabbinic Judaism, the written text of the Law. Under his leadership and tutelage the council replaced animal sacrifice with prayer and the temple with the synagogue and house of study, and he recommended that worship in the temple be replaced by benevolent deeds, all of which represented a creative advance; he gathered many relevant forms of worship and transformed the dominance of past laws into the firm foundation of a new era in Judaism. On the one hand, he preserved order amid the tragedy of loss—Jewish spiritual heritage, the Torah and its teachings; on the other hand, he infused the order with novelty—synagogue, prayer, and good deeds. Instead of being influenced by authority and scriptures, he influenced it in ways that brought it to new life. He saw the present in terms of the future: as shaping the future and passing into the future. It is tempting to think of God intervening in this process, since, as we learn from Whitehead that God and the world, in their natures, are in constant flux, in the grip of the creative advance into novelty. Each is the instrument of novelty for the other.

Ben Zakai's sensitivity towards the Jews' tragedy stemmed from his deep concern about the survival and future of his people. It is no surprise that he emphasized a good heart as the most important virtue and advocated peace among nations in the spirit of his master, Hillel. Ben Zakai's pragmatic approach and his tender feelings for new creations can be seen in his statement, "If you are holding a sapling in your hand and someone tells you, 'Come quickly, the messiah is here!' first finish planting the tree and then go to greet the messiah."[26] Akin to this is Muhammad's saying that on doomsday one should plant a palm shoot.

One of the great dangers for the Israelis and Palestinians is to think they can have a stalemate, which by nature doesn't exist; the essence of the universe is that there is either advance, the trend upward, or decay, the trend downward. These are the only choices available to the Palestinians and Israelis, the only choices in life. Palestinians, by resorting to murderous violence, and Israelis, by occupying Palestinian land with the humiliating

26. Rabbi Nathan, *Abot*, 31b.

consequences of roadblocks and checkpoints, degrade life and increase the danger of mutual destruction. Thus, to prevent further spiraling downwards and a widening of the chasm that already exists between the two peoples, discourse between them, however extreme and hostile, must be expanded to include persons of higher levels in both sides. The Israeli government will not engage in direct talks with Hamas unless it recognizes Israel, failing to see that diplomatic communication does not imply surrender. As is evident, insisting on preconditions for talks has been fruitless. Communication needs to be accompanied by the provision of incentives to Hamas to move towards stopping the violence against Israel. In addition, a plan for deterrence of violence by Israel should be put in place. Encouraging and promoting economic incentives in Palestine in general, such as proposals by the Palestine Investment Conference convened in May 2008, in Bethlehem, which encourage businessmen to invest in Palestine, could mitigate extremists' views. Pragmatic ideas that may be expressed even by those who as a rule think ideologically or on principle need to be highlighted and strengthened. No pragmatic idea, regardless of its origin, should go unnoticed.

Communication—using concerned speech, listening to the other, and expecting to be listened to—may lead to understanding the other, a necessary stage in discourse. As it is, each side is mistakenly certain they know the mind of the other, seeing the other as hostile and at fault rather than as having a different perspective of reality. For example, Israelis' beliefs, such as their right to the land based on the Bible and their history, refer to a reality that is meaningful only to the Jewish mind, and Palestinians' belief regarding their exclusive right to the land is meaningful only to the Palestinian mind. This fallacious either/or thinking often treats complex things as if they could be divided into simple extremes. As the philosopher S. Alexander points out, the process of opening minds to different facets of reality results in a new mental reality, recognition that the other's concerns are valid. This process of adapting minds to a new perspective of reality cannot be done easily or hurriedly. For one thing, each side is invested in their own limited knowledge of reality, and for another, the conflict belongs to a long history of injustices to both sides, which cannot be unraveled quickly. Opening up to the broader view of reality requires relinquishing this insular thinking. Nusseibeh invites Israel to "speak the language" of the Palestinians. He notes, "sensible people can easily arrive at a compromise

THE ISRAELI/PALESTINIAN CONFLICT

once they are aware of the other's basic concerns."[27] Such awareness can lead to sensitivity to the loss suffered by the other.

This sensitivity, the survival of the will to remedy the loss, turns the loss into a tragedy rather than an unmitigated evil. It allows the tragedy to disclose an ideal: "What might have been and was not: What can be. The tragedy was not in vain."[28] The tragedy will no longer be part of a vicious cycle, no longer part of the past, but rather capable of giving birth to a new reality. So far in this conflict, however, sensitivity to the other's concerns and the need for speaking the other's language has been limited to unofficial segments of both nations.

Nusseibeh provides an example of a remedy for Israelis to undertake. He stresses the significance of sulha in the Arab tradition, where the one that causes damage to another must apologize. In a talk to an Israeli audience he said:

> It doesn't matter whether you set out premeditatedly to cause the Palestinian refugee tragedy . . . the tragedy did occur even as an indirect consequence of your actions. In our tradition, you have to own up to this. You have to come and offer an apology. Only this way will Palestinians feel that their dignity has been recognized, and be able to forgive. But by denying all responsibility, besides being historically absurd to the point of craziness, you will guarantee eternal antagonism—a never-ending search for revenge.[29]

The sulha could be the initial step of reparation by Israel.

For their part in the conflict, Palestinians need to make reparation to Israel. However, they have a history of shirking responsibility. One instance is their refusal to recognize that the increasing and deepening of Israel's mistrust of them is based on experience: each time Israel gives up or returns land there is no decrease of violence on their part, and often an escalation. It is difficult to know who among the Palestinians—Nusseibeh, who expresses profound sensitivity to the Holocaust, and his colleagues seem to be an exception—is sensitive to the losses of Israelis and their own young people caused by suicide bombings. But many Palestinians, after learning of any kind of destruction inflicted on Israel, have been seen celebrating publicly, dancing and shooting in the air, ignoring the fact that fellow citizens have been wounded and killed. Thus, to remedy the damage on both

27. Nusseibeh, *Palestinian Life*, 321.
28. Whitehead, *Adventures*, 286.
29. Nusseibeh, *Palestinian Life*, 167.

sides, reparation is called for. The form of reparation cannot be dictated, but must be the creative product of the one who has done the damage. Once reparation takes place it enables reconciliation, which makes for a stronger relationship, just as a well-healed fractured bone is stronger than before the fracture.

In addition to direct talks, communication between the two nations can be established through education and dissemination of source material. Nusseibeh discusses reading about two philosophers of Jewish Viennese background who suffered humiliation and terror due to anti-Semitism. His empathy towards them is evident, and it demonstrates his capacity to step into another's shoes. In another instance he relates an exchange with his mother in which they both empathize with the devastating effect of persecution and humiliation on the Jews in Europe, and the need to make room for them in the land.

It is to be expected that the talks between Israelis and Palestinians will contain discord. Whitehead points out that a measure of discord is an evil that is impetus for creative advance. Though it always carries frustration, it "may be preferable to a feeling of slow relapse into general anesthesia, or into tameness which is its prelude."[30] The notion of discord brings to mind the thoughts of the poet William Blake: "Without Contraries is no progression. Attraction and Repulsion, Reason and Energy, Love and Hate, are necessary to Human existence."[31] That is, as Sir Geoffrey Keynes points out, "human thought and life need the stimulus of active and opposing forces to give them creative movement."[32] Obviously, the extreme discord between Israelis and Palestinians, which manifests itself in force and in violence, has been devastatingly destructive to the lives of both peoples. Yet the conflict in itself, by virtue of the opposition of feelings and thoughts, contains seeds of hope for a new life. This hope lies in the realization that discord as well as agreement in discussions among many minds is needed for truth to emerge. According to Alexander, it is only through the clashing of our judgments with those of others that we determine the truth or falsity of the propositions we consider and the worth of the ends we propose. Many minds put together are capable of extending their knowledge of reality by

---

30. Whitehead, *Adventures*, 263–64.
31. Blake, *Marriage*, xvi.
32. Ibid., xi.

piecing together the different perspectives; in this way they arrive at "fuller and higher or more perfect truths."[33]

It is paramount that all significant issues will be included in the Israeli-Palestinian dialogue—the disposition of Jerusalem, borders, the return of Arab refugees, and water. The language in the discourse must be precise and the meanings transparent. Nusseibeh, writing about the significance of words being precise, says he had always been aware of the dangers of hiding behind words. Arafat, former chairman of the PA, was a master at making meaningless and, at best, vague statements. He was noted for saying different things to different audiences. What he said in public in English almost never coincided with what he said in private, in Arabic, to his own people.

The success of negotiations between Israelis and Palestinians will require negotiators to allow their activity of thought, the progress of their investigation, to carry them, by a force outside themselves, to one and the same conclusion—not to where they wish but to an inevitable reality, what Peirce calls "fore-ordained"—by reasoning from the data. Success will be further contingent upon the adaptation of the representatives' minds to this new conclusion. This adaptation, requiring the extraordinary step of transcending tribal, group, and national identity, will form a common vision of survival and even of flourishing.

Successful discourse will produce "the collective mind . . . a short symbol for that cooperation and conflict of many minds which produces standards of approval or disapproval."[34] This mind is a kind of impartial spectator. Proposals that do not adhere to the standards agreed on will be rejected as errors—for example, actions that would produce hardships for the Palestinians, or actions that threaten the security of Israel. Proposals will be open to future amendments that guarantee the security and rights of the two nations in the future.

This collective mind as an impartial spectator will include the realization that the two peoples have a mutual interest in a better shared future; whatever is politically good for one must be good for the other. "Israelis and Palestinians, are not enemies at all," Nusseibeh said to an Israeli audience, "if anything we are strategic allies."[35] He noted that the Israelis think America is their ally, and the Palestinians think the Arab and Muslim world is their ally (whereas non-Palestinian Arabs have nothing but contempt for

---

33. Alexander, *Space, Time*, 264.
34. Ibid., 241.
35. Nusseibeh, *Palestinian Life*, 450.

the Palestinians, exploiting their plight to their own political advantage); but the truth is that Israelis and the Palestinians are allied. At its core this alliance, according to Nusseibeh, is a mysterious bond that connects the two peoples. This inherent bond is something that is felt but cannot be fully explained—a sense that both sides need to acknowledge; it is not a mere sentimental notion.

The Israeli and Palestinian nations, by virtue of this bond—by virtue of their living in proximity, their conflict, and their shared future—resonate with each other's experiences and affect the destiny of the other: when a desolation of spirit and a decline in values transpires in one nation, the other suffers as well; and any resolution that benefits one nation and not the other will ultimately affect both adversely. It is possible, by an act of the will, according to Nusseibeh, to perform a miracle even in this bloody conflict; the miracle would be turning hatred and enmity into understanding. It can be wrought out of the "throbbing emotion of the past," hurled, like the flying dart of Lucretius, beyond the bounds of the grief-stricken present, to create a future of reparation, cooperation, and a new beginning.

BIBLIOGRAPHY

Abravanel, Issac. Commentary in *Etz Hayim: Torah and Commentary*. David L. Lieber, senior editor. The Rabbinical Assembly, the United Synagogue of Conservative Judaism. New York: Jewish Publication Society, 2001.
Alexander, Samel. *Space, Time, and Deity*. Gifford Lectures, 1916–1918. Vol. 2. New York: Dover, 1966.
Arasteh, A. Rezi. *Rumi the Persian: Rebirth in Creativity and Love*. Pakistan: Rashmiri/Bazar, 1965.
Bachya ben Joseph ibn Paquda. *Duties of the Heart*. Vol. 2. Translated by Moses Hyamson. New York: Feldheim, 1986.
Bion, Wilfred R. *Cogitations*. Edited by Francesca Bion. London: Karnac, 1994.
Blake, William. *The Marriage of Heaven and Hell*. Introduction and commentary by Sir Geoffrey Keynes. New York: Oxford University Press, 1975.
Blyth, Reginald Horace. *Haiku*. 4 vols. Tokyo: Hokuseido, 1952. 21st printing, 1971.
Bollas, Christopher. *Forces of Destiny: Psychoanalysis and Human Idiom*. London: Free Association, 1991.
Bonhoeffer, Dietrich. *Letters and Papers from Prison*. Edited by Eberhard Bethge, translated by Reginald M. Fuller. New York: Macmillan, 1967.
Brandon, S. G. F., editor. *A Dictionary of Comparative Religion*. New York: Scribner's, 1970.
Buber, Martin. *I and Thou*. Translated by Walter Kaufmann. New York: Scribner's, 1970.
———. *Tales of the Hasidim*. Translated by Olga Marx. 2 vols. New York: Schocken, 1991.
Buchler, Justus, editor. *Philosophical Writings of Peirce*. New York: Dover, 1955.
Buddhaghosa, Bhadantacariya. *The Path of Purification*. Translated by Bhikkhu Nyanamoli. 2nd ed. Colombo, Ceylon: Semage, 1964.
Chang, Garma C. C., translator and annotator. *The Hundred Thousand Songs of Milarepa*. 2 vols. New Hyde Park, NY: University Books, 1962.
The Cloud of Unknowing. Translated with an introduction by Clifton Wolters. Baltimore: Penguin, 1970.
Cordovero, Rabbi Moshe. *The Palm Tree of Devorah*. Southfield, MI: Targun, 1993.
Corvan, Thomas G., translator. *The Best of Gracian*. New York: Philosophical Library, 1964.
Crawshay-Williams, Rupert. *Methods and Criteria of Reasoning: An Inquiry into the Structure of Controversy*. London: Routledge, 1957.
Dalai Lama. *The Dalai Lama, a Policy of Kindness : An Anthology of Writings by and about the Dalai Lama*. Compiled and edited by Sidney Piburn. Ithaca, NY: Snow Lion, 1990.

BIBLIOGRAPHY

Dawa-Samdup Lama Kazi. *Tibet's Great Yogi, Milarepa*. Edited by W. Y. Evans-Wentz. London: Oxford University Press, 1963.

Dhalla, Maneckji Nusservanji, translator and editor. *The Nyaishes or Zoroastrian Litanies: Khordah Avesta*. Columbia University Indo-Iranian Series, pt. 1, vol. 6. New York: AMS, 1965.

———. *Zoroastrian Theology: From the Earliest Times to the Present Day*. New York, 1914. Microfilm, University Microfilms International, ATLA monograph preservation program, ATLA fiche 1990–2043.

Duchesne-Guillemin, Jacques, translator. *The Hymns of Zarathustra*. London: John Murray, 1952.

Eigen, Michael. *Coming through the Whirlwind*. Wilmette, IL: Chiron, 1992.

———. *Contact with the Depths*. London: Karnac, 2011.

———. *Eigen in Seoul*. Vol. 2, *Faith and Transformation*. London: Karnac, 2011.

———. *The Electrified Tightrope*. Edited by Adam Phillips. . London: Karnac, 2004.

———. *Faith*. London: Karnac, 2014.

———. *Feeling Matters*. London: Karnac, 2007.

———. *Flames from the Unconscious: Trauma, Madness, and Faith*. London: Karnac, 2009.

———. Online workshop. 2013–.

———. *The Psychoanalytic Mystic*. London: Free Association, 1998.

———. *The Psychotic Core*. London: Karnac, 2004.

———. *The Sensitive Self*. Middletown, CT: Wesleyan University Press, 2004.

———. *Toxic Nourishment*. London: Karnac, 1999.

Emerson, Ralph Waldo. "The Over-Soul." In *The Complete Essays and Other Writings of Ralph Waldo Emerson*, 261–78. Edited by Brooks Atkinson. New York: Random House, 1950.

Evans-Wentz, W. Y., translator. *The Tibetan Book of the Great Liberation*. London: Oxford University Press, 1965.

Fingarette, Herbert. *Self-Deception*. Berkeley: University of California Press, 2000.

Finn, Mark. "Transitional Space and Tibetan Buddhism: The Object Relations of Meditation." In *Object Relations Theory and Religion: Clinical Applications*, edited by Mark Finn and John Gartner, 109–18. Westport, CT: Praeger, 1992.

Fremantle, Francesca, translator. *The Tibetan Book of the Dead*. Boston: Shambala, 2003.

Gandhi, Mohandas K. *An Autobiography: The Story of My Experiments with Truth*. Boston: Beacon, 1957.

Ghent, Emmanuel. "Masochism, Submission, Surrender: Masochism as a Perversion of Surrender." *Contemporary Psychoanalysis* 26 (1990) 108–36.

Gilliam, W. Craig. "A Half-Fast Walk through Martin Buber's Thinking." January 5, 2015. Online: http://justpeaceumc.org/a-half-fast-walk-through-martin-bubers-thinking/.

Gluck, Louise. "A Sharply Worded Silence." In *Faithful and Virtuous Night*, 19. New York: Fararr, Straus and Giroux, 2014.

Guntrip, Harry. *Psychoanalytic Theory, Therapy, and the Self*. New York: Basic Books, 1971.

Han Fei Tzu. *Basic Writings of Han Fei Tzu*. Translated by Burton Watson. New York: Columbia University Press, 1964.

Hass, Robert, editor and translator. *The Essential Haiku: Versions of Basho, Buson, & Issa*. New York: Ecco/HarperCollins, 1994.

BIBLIOGRAPHY

Hofmannsthal, Hugo von. *The Lord Chandos Letter*. Translated by Russell Stockman. Marlboro, VT: Marlboro, 1986.

Jacobs, Louis. *Hasidic Prayer*. New York: Schocken. 1978.

Jaeger, Werner. *Paideia: The Ideals of Greek Culture*. Vol. 1, *Archaic Greece, the mind of Athens*. Translated by Gilbert Highet. Oxford: Blackwell, 1954.

John of the Cross. *Dark Night of the Soul*. Translated and edited by E. Allison Peers, from the critical edition of P. Silverio de Santa Teresa. New York: Image, Doubleday, 1990.

———. *The Poems of St. John of the Cross*. Translated by Willis Barnstone. New York: New Directions, 1972.

Jones, Alexander, general editor. *The Jerusalem Bible*. Garden City, NY: Doubleday, 1966.

Kallus, Rabbi Menachem, translator and annotator. *The Pillar of Prayer: Guidance in Contemplative Prayer, Sacred Study, and the Spiritual Life, from the Baal Shem Tov and His Circle*. Louisville: Fons Vitae, 2011.

Kapitan, Tomis, editor. *Philosophical Perspectives on the Israeli-Palestinian Conflict*. Armonk, NY: Sharpe, 1997.

Kershner, Isabel. "Fatah Militants Lay Down Their Arms." *New York Times*, July 22, 2007.

Klein, Melanie. "Love, Guilt and Reparation." In *Love, Guilt, and Reparation, and Other Works, 1921–1945*, 311–43. New York: Free Press, 1975.

———. "On Mental Health." In *Envy and Gratitude and Other Works, 1946–1963*, 268–74. New York: Free Press, 1975.

———. "On the Sense of Loneliness." In ibid., 300–313. New York: Free Press, 1975.

Klein, Melanie, and Joan Riviere. *Love, Hate and Reparation*. New York: Norton, 1964.

Kook, Abraham Isaac. "Lights of Holiness." In *The Lights of Penitence, the Moral Principles, Lights of Holiness, Essays, Letters, and Poems*, translated by Ben Zion Bokser, 189–239. Ramsey, NJ: Paulist, 1978.

Kovner, Abba. "I don't know if Mount Zion." Translated by S. Kaufman. In *Voices within the Ark: The Modern Jewish Poets*, edited by Howard Schwartz & Anthony Rudolf, 117. New York: Avon, 1980.

Lagerkvist, Par. "The Basement." In *The Marriage Feast*, translated by Alan Blair, 63–71. New York: Hill and Wang, 1954.

Luzzatto, Moshe Chayim. *The Path of the Just*. Translated by Shraga Silverstein. New York: Feldheim, 1987.

Magid, Shaul. "Reb Zalman Schachter-Shalomi: The Holy Cobbler with a Secret." *Tikkun Daily*, July 8, 2014. Online: http://www.tikkun.org/tikkundaily/2014/07/08/reb-zalman-schachter-shalomi-the-holy-cobbler-with-a-secret/.

Masani, Sir Rustom Pestonji. *The Religion of the Good Life, Zoroastrianism*. London: Allen and Unwin, 1954.

Matt, Daniel C. *The Essential Kabbalah: The Heart of Jewish Mysticism*. San Francisco: HarperSanFrancisco, 1996.

McLean, Preston G. "Health: An Integrative Reticulum." *American Journal of Psychotherapy* 25/2 (1971) 300–308.

Merton, Thomas. *Contemplative Prayer*. New York: Doubleday, 1990.

Niebuhr, Reinhold. *Moral Man and Immoral Society: A Study in Ethics and Politics*. New York: Scribner's, 1960.

Nusseibeh, Sari, with Anthony David. *Once Upon a Country: A Palestinian Life*. New York: Farrar, Strauss, and Giroux, 2007.

Osborne, Arthur, editor. *Ramana Maharshi and the Path of Self-Knowledge*. London: Rider, 1963.

BIBLIOGRAPHY

Pagis, Dan. "Instructions for Crossing the Border." Translated by Stephen Mitchell. In *Voices within the Ark: The Modern Jewish Poets*, edited by Howard Schwartz & Anthony Rudolf, 130. New York: Avon, 1980.

Peirce, Charles S. *Philosophical Writings of Peirce*. Selected and edited by Justus Buchler. New York: Dover, 1955.

Plato. "Apology." In *The Dialogues of Plato*, translated by Benjamin Jowett, 1:401–23. New York: Random House, 1937.

———. "Crito." In ibid., 427–38.

———. "Phaedo." In ibid., 441–501.

Prentice, Robert P. *The Psychology of Love According to St. Bonaventure*. New York: Franciscan Institute of St. Bonaventure, 1957.

Rilke, Rainer Maria. "The Eighth Elegy." In *The Selected Poetry of Rainer Maria Rilke*, edited and translated by Stephen Mitchell, 193–97. New York: Random House, 1982.

———. "The First Elegy." In ibid., 151–55.

———. "Go to the Limits of Your Longing." Translated by Joanna Macy and Anita Barrows. Online: http://www.onbeing.org/program/wild-love-world/feature/go-limits-your-longing/1448.

———. "Letter 7." In *Letters to a Young Poet*, translated by Stephen Mitchell, 65–79. New York: Random House, 1986.

———. *Letters on Cezanne*. Edited by Clara Rilke, translated by Joel Agee. New York: Fromm, 1985.

———. "The Ninth Elegy." In *The Selected Poetry of Rainer Maria Rilke*, edited and translated by Stephen Mitchell, 199–203. New York: Random House, 1982.

———. "Requiem for a Friend." In ibid., 73–87.

———. "The Second Elegy." In ibid., 157–61.

Santayana, George. *Platonism and the Spiritual Life*. New York: Scribner's, 1927.

Scherman, Rabbi Nosson, translator and commentator. *The Complete ArtScroll Siddur*. New York: Me'sorah Pub., 1985.

Schneerson, Menachem M. *On the Essence of Chasidus*. New York: Kehot Pub. Society, 2013.

Schneur Zalman of Liadi. *Likutei Amarim Tanya: Bilingual Edition*. New York: Kehot Pub. Society, 1984.

Scholem, Gershom. *On the Kabbalah and Its Symbolism*. New York: Schocken, 1996.

Shah, Idries. *The Way of the Sufi*. New York: Arkana/Penguin, 1990.

Shavaksha, Gool K. S. *Zoroastrian Credo: The Life and Teachings of Zoroaster, the Gathas and Daily Prayers*. Bombay: Tripathi, 1962.

Simpson, Louis. *Three on the Tower: The Lives and Works of Ezra Pound, T. S. Eliot and William Carlos Williams*. New York: Morrow, 1975.

Sri Ramanasramam. *Talks with Sri Ramana Maharshi*. 3rd ed. Tiruvannamalai, S. India: T. N. Venkataraman, 1963.

Stein, Kenneth W. *The Land Question in Palestine, 1917–1939*. Chapel Hill: University of North Carolina Press, 1984.

Storr, Anthony. *Solitude: A Return to the Self*. New York: Ballantine, 1988.

Sultan, Sohaib N., annotator and translator. *The Qur'an and Sayings of Prophet Muhammad: Selections Annotated & Explained*. Woodstock, VT: Skylight Paths, 2007.

Tagore, Rabindranath. "The Crescent Moon." In *Collected Poems and Plays of Rabindranath Tagore*, 39–69. New York: Macmillan, 1973.

———. "Gitanjali." In ibid., 1–36.

BIBLIOGRAPHY

Teresa of Avila. *The Complete Works of Saint Teresa of Jesus*. Vol. 1. Translated and edited by E. Allison Peers, from the critical edition of P. Silverio de Santa Teresa. New York: Sheed & Ward, 1957.

Tillich, Paul. *The Courage to Be*. New Haven, CT: Yale University Press, 1968.

Whitehead, Alfred North. *Adventures of Ideas*. New York: Free Press, 1967.

———. *The Function of Reason*. Boston: Beacon, 1967.

———. *Process and Reality*. New York: Free Press, 1969.

———. *Religion in the Making*. New York: New American Library, 1974.

Williams, William Carlos. "The Red Wheelbarrow." In *The Norton Anthology of Modern Poetry*, edited by Richard Ellman and Robert O'Clair. New York: Norton, 1973.

Winnicott, D. W. *The Child, the Family, and the Outside World*. Hammondsworth, UK: Penguin, 1969.

———. "Communicating and Not Communicating Leading to a Study of Certain Opposites." In *The Maturational Processes and the Facilitating Environment: Studies in the Theory of Emotional Development*, 179–92. New York: International University Press, 1965.

———. "Cure." In *Home Is Where We Start From: Essays by a Psychoanalyst*, compiled and edited by Clare Winnicott, Ray Shepherd, Madeleine Davis, 112–20. New York: Norton, 1986.

———. "Ego Distortion in Terms of True and False Self." In *The Maturational Processes and the Facilitating Environment: Studies in the Theory of Emotional Development*, 140–52. New York: International University Press, 1965.

———. "Freedom." In *Home Is Where We Start From: Essays by a Psychoanalyst*, compiled and edited by Clare Winnicott, Ray Shepherd, Madeleine Davis, 228–38. New York: Norton, 1986.

———. *Human Nature*. New York: Schocken, 1988.

———. *The Maturational Processes and the Facilitating Environment*. New York: International University Press, 1965.

———. *Playing and Reality*. New York: Routledge, 1991.

———. "Psychoanalysis and the Sense of Guilt." In *The Maturational Processes and the Facilitating Environment: Studies in the Theory of Emotional Development*, 15–28. New York: International University Press, 1965.

———. "The Psycho-Somatic Field." In *Human Nature*, 26–29. New York: Schocken, 1988.

———. "The Value of Depression," In *Home Is Where We Start From: Essays by a Psychoanalyst*, compiled and edited by Clare Winnicott, Ray Shepherd, Madeleine Davis, 71–79. New York: Norton, 1986.

Zaehner, R. C. *The Teachings of the Magi: A Compendium of Zoroastrian Beliefs*. New York: Oxford University Press, 1976.

www.ingramcontent.com/pod-product-compliance
Lightning Source LLC
Chambersburg PA
CBHW050832160426
43192CB00010B/2000